RIDE GUIDE

Hudson Valley
New Paltz to Staten Island

2nd Edition
By Dan Goldfischer

White Meadow Press

RIDE GUIDE Hudson Valley New Paltz to Staten Island
Second Edition
Copyright 1996 by Daniel Goldfischer

Cover: *photo by Daniel Goldfischer; design by Andrea Burke.*

Illustrations: *Kathy Murray*

ISBN 0-933855-10-9
Library of Congress Catalog Card Number: 96-61364

Also available
Bed, Breakfast & Bike New England
Bed, Breakfast & Bike Mid-Atlantic
Bed, Breakfast & Bike Northern California
Bed, Breakfast & Bike Pacific Northwest
RIDE GUIDE North Jersey 2nd Edition
RIDE GUIDE Central Jersey

Send for our catalog:
Anacus Press, Inc.
P.O. Box 4544
Warren, NJ 07059

Published by
<u>WHITE MEADOW PRESS</u>
a Division of

P. O. Box 4544, Warren, New Jersey 07059

"Ride Guide" and "Bed Breakfast & Bike" are trademarks of Anacus Press, Inc.

Printed in the United States of America

ACKNOWLEDGMENTS

Thanks to the readers and supporters of this book, many of whom I have met on the road or at GEAR rallies over the past 10 years.

Thanks to my new publishers, Albert and Gail Knight of Anacus Press, for keeping the RIDE GUIDE tradition alive.

Thanks to my parents, Lester and Marion Goldfischer, for assistance in research.

Thanks to my wife Sharlene and my son Eric for their patience and love during my years of scouting, researching and writing about bike routes.

CONTENTS

RIDE GUIDE
ROUTE STARTING POINTS

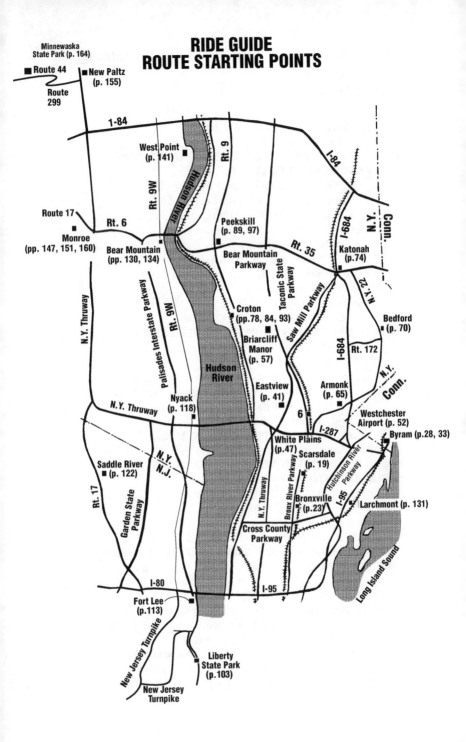

Minnewaska State Park (p. 164)
Route 44
New Paltz (p. 155)
Route 299
I-84
West Point (p. 141)
Rt. 9
Rt. 9W
Hudson River
I-84
N.Y.
Conn.
I-684
Route 17
Rt. 6
Peekskill (p. 89, 97)
Rt. 35
Katonah (p. 74)
Monroe (pp. 147, 151, 160)
Bear Mountain (pp. 130, 134)
Bear Mountain Parkway
N.Y. 22
Taconic State Parkway
Saw Mill Parkway
N.Y. Thruway
Palisades Interstate Parkway
Rt. 9W
Croton (pp. 78, 84, 93)
Bedford (p. 70)
Briarcliff Manor (p. 57)
I-684
Rt. 172
Hudson River
Eastview (p. 41)
Armonk (p. 65)
N.Y.
Conn.
Nyack (p. 118)
N.Y. Thruway
6
Westchester Airport (p. 52)
I-287
Byram (p. 28, 33)
White Plains (p. 47)
Saddle River (p. 122)
N.Y.
N.J.
Scarsdale (p. 19)
Hutchinson River Parkway
Rt. 17
Garden State Parkway
Bronx River Parkway
N.Y. Thruway
Bronxville (p. 23)
I-95
Larchmont (p. 131)
Cross County Parkway
Long Island Sound
I-80
I-95
Fort Lee (p. 113)
New Jersey Turnpike
Liberty State Park (p. 103)
New Jersey Turnpike

INTRODUCTION

It **has** been 10 years since the original *RIDE GUIDE/Hudson Valley and Sound Shore* appeared. Like everywhere else in the United States, the region covered by this book has grown, become more congested with cars and houses and more urban in general.

Yet the Hudson Valley retains its peaceful beauty, thanks to the foresight of New York State parks planners and the wealth of some of its historic families, including the Rockefellers. In many places it is truly the land of Rip Van Winkle, the land that time forgot. And that's what makes bicycle touring such an ideal way to see the area — you can see things at a slow pace, up close and personal in a way not possible in an automobile.

Picture yourself riding under soaring peaks, the majesty of the mighty river far below down the cliff. Or perhaps cycling down bucolic suburban streets near Long Island Sound, passing the mighty mansions of older Westchester communities. Perhaps the still-wild woods of the north country "hollows" is more your style. All these cycling experiences are available within a 90-minute car or train ride from New York City.

If off-road riding is your preference, **RIDE GUIDE Hudson Valley New Paltz to Staten Island** includes four of the best areas in the region for fat-tire enthusiasts. Trails range from the tricky terrain of Blue Mountain Reservation to the mecca of miles of carriage roads at Minnewaska State Park.

Along the way, there's sure to be swimming holes, museums, historic houses and photogenic viewpoints to stop at. Bicycling **RIDE GUIDE** style is more than pushing the pedals — it is the whole slow-paced touring experience of enjoying and learning about a region.

Welcome to **RIDE GUIDE Hudson Valley New Paltz to Staten Island**. Read the next section on **How To Use This Book**, pack the guide in your pack or handlebar bag and away you go! See you on the road.

HOW TO USE THIS BOOK

*R*IDE GUIDE *Hudson Valley New Paltz to Staten Island* is organized by sections according to route starting points. Thus, Central Westchester includes rides heading into Northern Westchester, and some routes in the Lower Hudson Valley head toward the Mid-Hudson Valley. The name of each route generally consists of the point of origin and a major destination. All routes return to their starting points. Directions are often given for combining routes to make longer tours. Read the section introductions for summaries of routes within each section. Sections and rides within sections are presented in the book in rough geographic order, from south to north and east to west. The sections entitled Lower Hudson Valley and Mid-Hudson Valley cover routes starting on the west side of the river.

Readers of the first edition of this book will note the coverage area of this edition of **RIDE GUIDE** has been expanded north to include Ulster County, mainly because of the beautiful area near New Paltz, mecca for outdoor recreationalists. Also, this edition contains clearly identified off-road rides.

Getting closer to deciding where to ride? If you are an experienced cycle tourist, points of interest may be the deciding factor. Carless cyclists should pay attention to Metro-North directions, which indicate how close ride starting points are to train stations. Novice and intermediate riders should closely examine the following factors, all listed in capsule descriptions at the beginning of each route chapter:

Mileage: If you've never ridden more than 20 miles in a day, it might not be a good idea to jump into a 50-mile ride, but you should be able to handle 25 or 30 miles. If you've overestimated your ability, the map will offer short-cuts back to the starting point.

Terrain: Far more important than how far you are going is what kind of terrain you will experience. The Hudson Valley and interior Westchester and Fairfield counties are hilly to various degrees, and the capsule descriptions state whether a route is gently rolling or "memorably challenging." Decide what you can handle, then challenge yourself a little! It is not a disgrace to walk your bike up a hill when you are tired.

Traffic: Road routes can become less than enjoyable if there are a lot of cars competing for your space. While every effort is made to keep routes on quiet roads, sometimes short distances on busy thoroughfares are unavoidable, and this is noted here. The "traffic" section of ATB routes refers to how many other trail users (mostly hikers) you will encouter.

Road Conditions: For road routes, this descriptor tells you whether there are large numbers of potholes or stretches of dirt along the way. Even the skinniest-tire road enthusiast should slow down and enjoy a dirt road once in a while. ATB routes incorporate a Trail Conditions description, telling you whether to expect hard-packed dirt or challenging rocks and logs.

Now you've picked a ride and are ready to go. **Directions to Starting Point** tells you how to get there by car, and **Metro-North Directions** will tell you how to arrive at the starting point by train (only on the east side of the Hudson, however, and for rides leaving from Bear Mountain and West Point). To obtain the permit necessary for bringing a bike on a commuter train, go to any Metro-North ticket window or Window 27 at Grand Central Terminal, or call 212-532-4900. A $5 lifetime fee is charged, and bikes are not permitted on rush-hour trains in the rush-hour direction.

Be sure you have packed all the necessary water, food, clothing and bike repair equipment recommended in all excellent books on bicycle touring, and, along with RIDE GUIDE, pack a local or regional map. The reason for the map is road patterns sometimes change after guidebooks such as this are published (even route numbers and street names can change), and it is helpful to have the latest possible information.

The maps in this book should be used for general orientation, as they are not drawn to scale. Use the cue sheet to determine the next street or landmark.

How to Use The Cue Sheets: The two columns of mileage figures are point to point (left column), which represents the distance from the previous turn or landmark, and cumulative (right column), which represents the distance from the starting point.

Abbreviations in the turns column are:

L	Left
R	Right
S	Straight
BL	Bear Left
BR	Bear Right
SL	Sharp Left
SR	Sharp Right

In the **streets/landmarks** column, only the street you are supposed to be on is printed in **boldface**. Intersecting roads are printed in lightface. Italics are used to indicate directions to connecting routes.

A **(T)** is an intersection where the road you are on ends at another road. You must go right or left; you cannot go straight.

All the rides in this book have been researched by the author and are described in detail. However, conditions change: road maintenance deteriorates; trails erode; traffic patterns change; signs disappear, etc. Hence, there is no guarantee that the conditions described herein will exist at a later date. Cycle with caution, wear your helmet and use common sense.

RIDES STARTING IN SOUTHERN WESTCHESTER AND NEARBY CONNECTICUT

Old-time New York City residents still think of anything north of Fordham Road in the Bronx as "the country" or "upstate." Inhabitants of more northerly locales such as Yorktown or North Salem picture downtown Mt. Vernon and Yonkers when they think of Southern Westchester and equate the entire section with New York City. The reality is somewhere in between: while Southern Westchester has its busy cities and crowded thoroughfares, there is still plenty of pleasant, almost country-like cycling to be had in this section, particularly in the wealthier towns.

Cycling in Southern Westchester means quiet suburban streets with large homes of every architectural style: New York City's corporate executives have been commuting from Westchester for over a century and it is only recently that tracts of look-alike homes have been built. Rye, Scarsdale, Larchmont, Pelham and Greenwich in particular have some real palaces and castles.

This section features Long Island Sound, a large salt-water inland sea known as the "Times Square of recreational boating". On a good summer weekend you can have difficulty seeing the water for all the sailboats on the Sound, and the views of coves, waterside homes and natural landmarks and wildlife, along with Long Island across the way, are very photogenic. Nature lovers appreciate the marshland and saltwater bird life of the Sound Shore area, and there are several good places to view the marshes.

For the cyclist, Southern Westchester and nearby Connecticut mean flat and fairly easy going near the Sound, and a bit hillier inland, particularly in Greenwich. **Sound Shore Wanderer**, rerouted from the first edition, goes south from Larchmont and heads to the very neck of the sound — Throgs Neck, to be precise, with its impressive view of bridges and Manhattan towers. The return includes City Island, a seafood lovers' paradise, and numerous water views and beaches.

Scarsdale-Playland starts inland and reaches the water at Mamaroneck. Stops enroute to Playland include Marshlands, a fantastic nature preserve where woods meet water and egrets nest in marshes. And anyone who grew up in the area knows the magic of Playland, the art-deco masterpiece of old-time amusement parks.

Westchester's county government has been encouraging cycling since the mid-70s by closing off the Bronx River Parkway for four hours on many Sundays. Although budgetary restrictions have prevented bicycle Sundays from taking place every Sunday, private sponsorship by the Freihofer bakery among others have allowed this wonderful event to occur almost every Sunday in May, June and September. Autos are banished from Tuckahoe to White Plains from 10 AM to 2 PM, allowing cyclists to enjoy the lush greenery of America's first landscaped parkway, a national historic site. For riders who want to enjoy this serene strip located in a very densely populated corridor but don't want to wait until a bicycle Sunday, **Bronx River Valley** presents parallel routes to the parkway on quiet residential streets and bike paths.

Greenwich is one of the wealthiest towns in the U.S. It is also a cyclist's paradise with its varied and interesting terrain ranging from Sound flat to New England inland hilly. The roads are quiet and well-paved, with occasional country stores for fuel along the way. **Greenwich Sampler** includes a little inland hilly and a little Sound (relatively) flat, and **Greenwich-Armonk** is more challenging in terms of terrain, and gets farther out into the remote "back country" of large estates and horse farms. The latter route includes stops at the outdoor sculpture garden at Pepsico headquarters, the state university at Purchase, N.Y. and Westchester County Airport.

Southern Westchester and nearby Connecticut have something for every cyclist to enjoy. City slickers can find country riding close by (in Greenwich), while riders used to farms and woods may wish to gaze at large homes by Long Island Sound. Enjoy!

SOUND SHORE WANDERER - 36.4 MILES

Terrain: Mostly flat, since this ride follows the shore of Long Island Sound.
Traffic: Urban traffic can be expected in a few places, moderate elsewhere. There is surprisingly little traffic south of Pelham Bay Park to Throgs Neck.
Road Conditions: Fair to good, except some potholes in the city sections.
Points of Interest: Large homes in Larchmont, Pelham and parts of New Rochelle; **Bartow-Pell Mansion** (restored historic home); **view of New York City and bridges** from Throgs Neck; City Island (seafood restaurants and shops); Sound Shore parks: **Manor Park, Hudson Park, Orchard Beach, and Glen Island.**

Long **Island Sound** does not play as important part in American history as the Hudson Valley does, but it is definitely worth exploration if only for the spectacular water views and the salt air.

This route covers a populous area and some parts of the ride go over busy streets, so riders should brush up on their defensive cycling skills. But mingled with the unavoidable urban thoroughfares are quiet suburban roads with huge homes, a New England fishing village located within the borders of New York City, and fine waterside parks.

Start by the Larchmont railroad station and make a bee-line for Long Island Sound down a tree-lined road of fine, old mansions. In less than two miles you are enjoying the first of many fine views of Long Island Sound and exploring Manor Park. Note that Manor Park as well as some of the other parks visited along this route are technically open only to residents of the community, but generally cyclists are not hassled, especially outside of busy summer weekends.

A bit of urban riding takes you into New Rochelle, where you visit Hudson Park. A side trip is available to the Wildcliff Art Center. Quieter roads take you by the College of New Rochelle, the oldest Catholic women's college in New York State. Pass some more huge mansions in Pelham before heading south into the Bronx.

Your goal is to reach SUNY Maritime, directly under the Throgs Neck Bridge, with its impressive view of water, the Manhattan skyline, other bridges and planes approaching LaGuardia Airport.

SOUND SHORE WANDERER
36.4 Miles

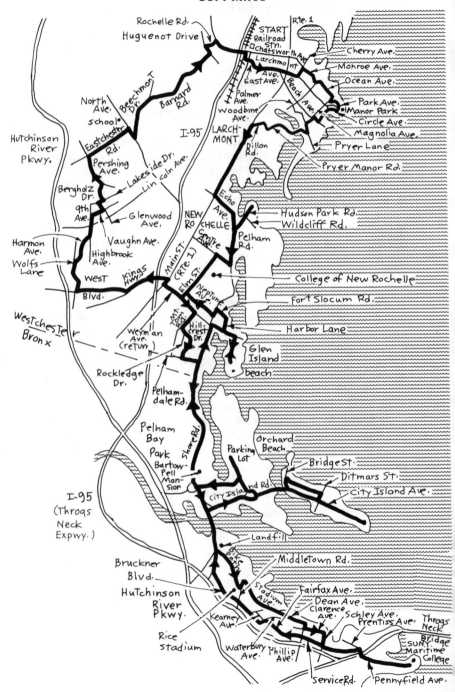

Enroute you will ride through Pelham Bay Park and down quiet, clean and safe residential streets that characterize this section of the Bronx.

The return from Throgs Neck takes you to City Island, a unique collection of boats, seafood restaurants and antique shops. The entire island is only two blocks wide!

The return from the Bronx, new for this edition of *RIDE GUIDE*, takes you inland through areas of fine, large homes and quiet streets of smaller old homes in Pelham Manor and New Rochelle before returning to the Larchmont Station.

Swimming is available at Orchard Beach, Glen Island and Hudson Park, and the cool salt water is wonderfully refreshing on a hot day. Bring a sturdy lock if planning to leave your bike anywhere, and take your valuables off your bike. Plenty of food is available along this route.

Directions to Starting Point: The ride starts at the **Larchmont Station** of Metro-North. By car, take Exit 17 off I-95 north, just past the New Rochelle toll booth. Continue straight ahead to the second stop sign and turn right on Chatsworth Ave. Cross over highway and railroad and turn left. Parking is available in lots near the station. From I-95 south, use exit 18B, Mamaroneck Ave. South. Drive one mile and turn right just past the railroad overpass. Bear right onto Palmer Ave. and drive two miles into Larchmont. Turn right in the center of Larchmont at Chatsworth Ave., and right again into the railroad station parking area.
Metro-North Directions: Take a New Haven Line Stamford local to Larchmont. Carry your bike up the stairs at the rear of the platform to Chatsworth Ave. and the start of the ride.

Pt. to Point	Cume	Turn	Street/Landmark
0.0	0.0		From Chatsworth Ave. and the Connecticut-bound side of the railroad station, cross Chatsworth Ave. onto **North Ave.**, a small one-way street paralleling the railroad
0.1	0.1	L	**East Ave.**
0.1	0.2	S	Cross Palmer Ave. at traffic light onto **Larchmont Ave.**
0.5	0.7	S	Cross Route 1

Pt. to Point	Cume	Turn	Street/Landmark
0.1	0.8	L	**Cherry Ave**
0.1	0.9	R	**Monroe Ave.** (stop sign)
0.3	1.2	L	**Woodbine Ave.** (stop sign)
0.0	1.2	R	**Ocean Ave.**
0.3	1.5	R	**Magnolia Ave.** (first of many views of Long Island Sound)
0.0	1.5	L	**Park Ave.** (one-way street)
0.2	1.7		**Manor Park** on left
0.0	1.7	L	**Circle Ave.** (one-way; stay left at fork)
0.1	1.8	L	**Park Ave.**
0.3	2.1	R	**Beach Ave.**
0.1	2.2	L	**Magnolia Ave.**
0.1	2.3	L	**Pryer Lane**
0.1	2.4	R	**Pryer Manor Rd.** (very winding, with up hill at end)
0.6	3.0	S	Becomes **Dillon Rd.**
0.1	3.1	L	**Boston Post Rd. (Rt. 1)**
1.1	4.2	L	**Echo Ave.** (Pizza Hut on corner)
0.4	4.6	R	**Pelham Road** (curve right)
0.2	4.8	SL	**Hudson Park Rd.** (traffic light)
0.1	4.9		Turn right at Wildcliff Rd. for **Wildcliff Art Center**
0.3	5.2		**U-turn** at end of parking lot in **Hudson Park**. Then return along **Hudson Park Rd.**
0.4	5.6	L	**Pelham Road**
0.4	6.0	R	**Centre Ave.** (at Isaac Young school)
0.2	6.2	L	**Elm St.** (traffic light). **College of New Rochelle** will be on the left shortly after the turn
0.6	6.8	L	**Weyman Ave.** (T)
0.2	7.0	R	**Mt. Tom Rd.**
0.6	7.6	L	**Rockledge Dr.** (stop sign)
0.2	7.8	R	**Hillcrest Dr.** (T)
0.4	8.2	L	**Pelhamdale Ave.** (T)
0.3	8.5	R	**Shore Rd.** (T)
1.2	9.7		**Bartow-Pell Mansion** on left
0.4	10.1	S	Go halfway around the traffic circle toward **City Island-Shore Road South**
0.9	11.0	L	Carefully cross road near landfill (on left) and ride onto the service road (near landfill), against traffic
0.2	11.2	L	Enter bike path in **Pelham Bay Park.**

Pt. to Point	Cume	Turn	Street/Landmark
			Head south on the paths toward **Rice Stadium**
0.9	12.1	L	**Middletown Rd.** after exiting bike path in front of Rice Stadium
0.1	12.2	R	**Stadium Ave.**
0.8	13.0	BR	At fork onto **Dean Ave.** (Prospect Rest Nursing Home on left)
0.4	13.4	R	**Philip Ave.** (curve right)
0.0	13.4	L	**Clarence Ave.**
0.4	13.8	R	**Schley Ave.** (curve right)
0.1	13.9	L	**Throgs Neck Expwy. (service road)** (stop sign)
0.6	14.5	R	**Prentiss Ave.** (stop sign). Cross highway
0.3	14.8	BL	At traffic light onto **Pennyfield Ave.** (toward SUNY Maritime College)
0.6	15.4		**SUNY Maritime College** on left. Sign in at guardhouse to ride through college (views of Manhattan, water and bridges). Return the way you came on **Pennyfield Ave.**
0.9	16.3	BR	At traffic light to cross over highway
0.0	16.3	L	**Throgs Neck Expwy. (service road)**
0.7	17.0	L	At stop sign and T to continue on **Throgs Neck Expwy. (service road)**
0.6	17.6	S	At stop sign onto **Fairfax Ave.**; continue to parallel highway
0.3	17.9	L	**Waterbury Ave.** (T)
0.1	18.0	R	**Kearney Ave.** (T). After turn go straight on **service road (Bruckner Blvd.)** which parallels highway (Kearney Ave. bears right)
0.5	18.5	BL	To continue on service road (Pelham Bay Park is on the right)
0.5	19.0	BR	Toward **Orchard Beach and City Island**
1.0	20.0	R	At traffic light (toward **City Island**) after passing drawbridge
0.7	20.7	S	Go halfway around traffic circle toward **City Island**
0.7	21.4	BR	After going over bridge onto **City Island Ave.**
1.3	22.7		**U-turn** at end of **City Island Ave.**
0.9	23.6	R	**Ditmars St.**
0.1	23.7	L	**Minnieford Ave.**

Pt. to Point	Cume	Turn	Street/Landmark
0.5	24.2	L	**Bridge St.** (street sign on right hidden under tree branch)
0.1	24.3	R	Cross bridge
0.6	24.9	R	At traffic circle toward **Orchard Beach**
0.8	25.7		**U-turn** at **Orchard Beach**
0.7	26.4	R	Toward **Hutchinson River Pkwy.**
0.3	26.7	R	At traffic circle onto **Shore Rd. North**
2.3	29.0	R	At traffic light, toward **Glen Island**
0.2	29.2	S	Cross bridge onto **Glen Island**
0.5	29.7		Circle island and return over the draw bridge
0.5	30.2	R	**Harbor Lane**
0.1	30.3	L	**Ft. Slocum Rd.** (T) (no sign)
0.2	30.5	L	**Pelham Rd.** (T) (no sign)
0.0	30.5	R	**Neptune Ave.**
0.4	30.9	L	**Elm St.** (traffic light)
0.1	31.0	R	**Weyman Ave.** (T)
0.2	31.2	R	**Main St.** (Rt. 1)
0.1	31.3	SL	**Kings Highway** (traffic light)
0.4	31.7	BR	**West Boulevard** (stop sign at end of cemetery)
0.7	32.4	R	**Wolfs Lane** (traffic light)
0.3	32.7	R	**Harmon Ave.** (second right turn after going under railroad)
0.5	33.2	L	**Highbrook Ave.**
0.1	33.3	S	Cross Lincoln Ave. at traffic light onto 9th Ave.
0.2	33.5	R	**Vaughn Ave.**
0.2	33.7	L	**Glenwood Ave.**
0.1	33.8	R	**Lakeside Dr.**
0.0	33.8	L	**Bergholz Dr.**
0.1	33.9	BL	**Pershing Ave.**
0.3	34.2	R	**Eastchester Rd.** (traffic light)
0.6	34.8	R	**North Ave.** (T; New Rochelle High School on left)
0.0	34.8	L	**Beechmont Dr.** (traffic light; winding uphill)
0.8	35.6	R	**Barnard Rd.** (across from Beechmont Lake; goes downhill)
0.3	35.9	L	**Huguenot Dr.** (steep uphill at end)
0.0	35.9	R	**Rochelle Rd.**
0.1	36.0	R	**Chatsworth Ave.**
0.4	36.4		**Larchmont Station** on left (end of route)

SCARSDALE-PLAYLAND - 29.5 MILES

Terrain: Gently rolling. Some longer climbs out of the Bronx River Valley and heading inland from the Sound.
Traffic: Mostly quiet suburban streets, with some short stretches on busier roads.
Road Conditions: Very good, except bumpy Griffen Rd.
Points of Interest: Large homes; Harbor views in Mamaroneck and Rye; **Marshlands Conservancy** (hiking and nature exhibit); **Rye Beach; Playland Amusement Park; Square House** of Rye Historical Society.

Southern **Westchester**, while being for the most part an urban, built-up section of suburban New York, does have its quieter parts. The wealthy towns of Scarsdale, Mamaroneck, Rye and Harrison have broad, smooth roads with large estates, sections of undeveloped woods and even a horse farm or two.

Playland, destination of this route, is the finest example of an art-deco amusement park in the U.S. Located on the Sound, the flower-lined midway capped by the tall music tower is etched into many a Westchesterite's memory. The county-run attraction is still a fun and free place to visit, and cycling there beats the cost and hassle of parking. Try out the legendary Dragon Coaster for some thrilling terrain.

On the way to Playland, be sure to stop at Marshlands Conservancy. The nature preserve has a beautiful trail leading through woods to wetlands by the Sound, where waterbirds such as egrets and great blue herons can be observed.

Rye Beach is an excellent swimming beach, but is generally reserved for town residents and their guests. Swimming is available at Playland.

Directions to Starting Point: This route begins at the intersection of **East Parkway and Popham Rd.** in downtown Scarsdale. Take the Bronx River Pkwy. to Exit 12 and proceed along East Parkway to the traffic light, which is Popham Rd. Metered parking is available on village streets; longer-term parking can be found in a garage across the railroad tracks and south of the train stations.
Metro-North Directions: Take a Harlem Line White Plains North

SCARSDALE-PLAYLAND
29.5 Miles

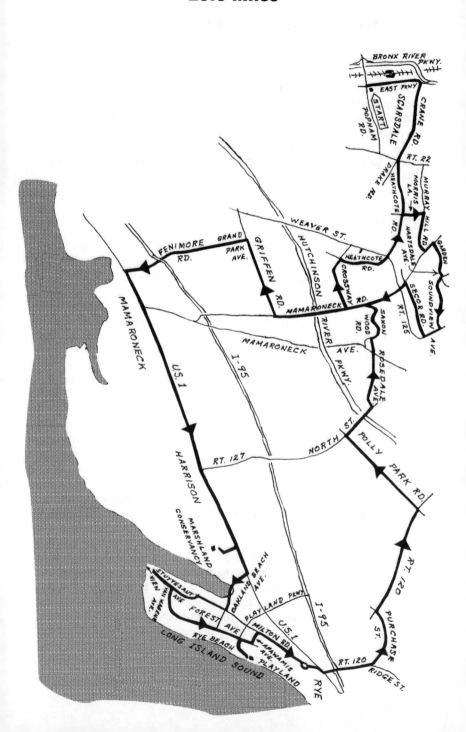

local to Scarsdale. Carry your bike up the rear stairs on the platform, which lead to Popham Rd. (the street which crosses over the streets). East Parkway is to your left, paralleling the railroad). _Note: This route may be combined with the Bronx River Valley ride (p.23) to make a 57-mile route. On Bicycle Sundays (see section introduction), you cannot drive on the Bronx River Pkwy. Park your car in Bronxville and ride up the Parkway to Scarsdale to begin the route. This will add 8 miles to the round-trip distance._

Pt. to Point	Cume	Turn	Street/Landmark
0.0	0.0		Start at the intersection of **East Park way and Popham Rd**. With your back to the railroad, turn **left** on **East Parkway.**
0.2	0.2	R	**Crane Rd.**
0.6	0.8	BL	**Heathcote Rd.** (cross Rt. 22)
0.8	1.6	L	**Morris Lane** (traffic light)
0.6	2.2	R	**Murray Hill Rd.** (T)
0.4	2.6	L	**Mamaroneck Rd.** (traffic light)
0.4	3.0	R	**Garden Rd.**
0.5	3.5	S	At stop sign. Road changes name to **Hartsdale Ave.** at White Plains city line
0.2	3.7	R	**Soundview Ave.** (traffic light)
0.6	4.3	R	**Old Mamaroneck Rd. (Rt. 125)** (traffic light)
0.8	5.1	R	**Secor Rd.**
0.3	5.4	L	**Mamaroneck Rd.** (traffic light)
0.6	6.0	BL	At fork to continue on **Mamaroneck Rd.** (Crossway goes right)
0.9	6.9	R	**Griffen Rd.** (at end of stone wall)
1.1	8.0	L	**Grand Park Ave.** (which shortly changes name to **Fenimore Rd.**)
2.2	10.2	L	**Boston Post Rd. (Rt. 1)** (T)
1.3	11.5		Farm stand on right
0.7	12.2	R	Into driveway of **Marshlands Conservancy**
0.2	12.4		Start of hiking trail to Long Island Sound. After hiking, cycle back the way you came in (water and restrooms are available here)
0.2	12.6	R	**Rt. 1** (T)
0.6	13.2	R	**Oakland Beach Ave.** (traffic light)
0.6	13.8	R	**Milton Rd.** (traffic light) (store on right shortly after turn)
0.5	14.3	L	**Stuyvesant Ave.** (blinking light)

Pt. to Point	Cume	Turn	Street/Landmark
1.1	15.4		**U-turn** by entrance to American Yacht Club (end of public road). Enjoy the view of Milton Harbor!
0.5	15.9	R	**Van Wagenen Ave.**
0.2	16.1	L	**Forest Ave.** (curve left)
0.9	17.0		Entrance to **Rye Beach** on right
0.4	17.4	R	**Playland Pkwy.** (traffic light)
0.3	17.7		**Playland** entrance. Return the way you came in
0.4	18.1	R	**Forest Ave.** (traffic light)
0.3	18.4	L	**Apawamis Ave.** (traffic light)
0.4	18.8	R	**Milton Rd.** (T)
0.6	19.4	L	At traffic circle to continue on **Milton Rd.**
0.1	19.5	S	At traffic light, onto **Rt. 1 North**
0.0	19.5	BL	At fork (immediately after last turn) onto **Purchase St. (Rt. 120).** To see the **Square House** of the Rye Historical Society, make a sharp left onto Haviland Lane
0.8	20.3	S	At red blinking light to continue on **Purchase St. (Rt. 120)**. (Ridge St. goes right)
0.5	20.8	R	At red blinking light to continue on **Rt. 120**
0.6	21.4	L	**Polly Park Rd.** (traffic light)
1.6	23.0	R	**North St. (Rt. 127)** (traffic light)
0.4	23.4	L	**Rosedale Ave.**
1.2	24.6	S	Cross Mamaroneck Ave. at traffic light
0.2	24.8	R	**Saxon Wood Rd.** (T)
1.3	26.1	L	**Mamaroneck Rd.** (T)
0.2	26.3	BR	At fork onto **Crossway**
0.5	26.8	R	**Heathcote Rd.**
0.5	27.3	S	Cross Palmer Ave. at 5-way traffic light
1.4	28.7	BR	**Crane Rd.** (cross Rt. 22)
0.6	29.3	L	**East Parkway**
0.2	29.5		Intersection of **East Parkway and Popham Rd.** (end of route)

BRONX RIVER VALLEY - 24.0 MILES

As **noted** in the introduction to this section, Westchester County closes seven miles of the Bronx River Pkwy. to auto traffic for several hours on a number of Sundays during the fine-weather cycling months of May, June, and September. What about cyclists who wish to ride in this pretty area when only autos may use the parkway? This route presents parallel roads and bike paths that follow the Bronx River Valley. It is described in narrative format rather than a cue sheet because there are so many turns in such a short distance.

Even if the parkway is closed to cyclists, it is a pleasure cycling here because of the many paths that allow you to see America's first landscaped parkway, a registered historic landmark. When there are no paths, quiet suburban roads lined with fine old homes constitute the alternate route. The endpoint is Kensico Dam Plaza, a fine park which often hosts festivals and musical events. Cyclists can ride up and over the dam, returning to the park on a zooming downhill.

Directions To Starting Point: Bronxville Station is located off the Bronx River Pkwy. Take the Pondfield Rd. exit from the northbound parkway and turn right. From the southbound parkway, turn right on Scarsdale Rd., left on Parkview Ave., then left on Pondfield Rd. and proceed to the station, where metered parking is available.
Metro-North Directions: Take a Harlem Division local bound for North White Plains to the Bronxville station.
Note: Two other rides in this guide start at places along this route: Scarsdale-Playland (page 19) and North White Plains-Usonia (page 47).

Start at the **Bronxville Station** and pedal west on **Pondfield Rd.** (toward the Bronx River Pkwy.). Signs on the traffic circle on the New York-bound side of the station will identify the correct road. Shortly before Pondfield Rd. crosses the parkway, turn right on either of **two bike** path spurs. After a short, steep rise and fall, both spurs join to form one path, then separate again at the bottom of a duck pond. Choose the path on the **right side of the pond** (crossing a footbridge immediately). This will enable you to avoid carrying your bike up stairs at Tuckahoe Rd. The pond and lawns are popular in season with local fowl-feeders and sun-bathers.

The path crosses Tuckahoe Rd. as the road forks to enter Tuckahoe. Look closely for fast-moving traffic as you cross this street. Next the path runs on a striped-off area of the **Elm St. on-ramp** to the parkway before continuing on its own separate right of way.

At **Scarsdale Rd.** you have reached the southern end of the Bronx River Pkwy. closing area, and if you happen to be here between 10 and 2 of a bicycle Sunday, take to the highway. If not, continue on the path, which crosses a couple of residential streets before appearing to backtrack in order to cross a stream at the bottom of another duck pond. You will ride alongside this pond for a ways. Take the left fork to stay closer to the river as you approach the **Crestwood railroad station.**

After crossing the entrance road to the station parking lot, the path follows a driveway leading to a parkway maintenance garage, then returns to its own right of way. The next two miles to the end of the path at Harney Rd. has only one road crossing, and bridges the Bronx River several times.

Carefully cross Harney Rd. at path's end onto **Garth Rd.** (do not cross the parkway or railroad). This street features fine old Tudor apartment houses. At the traffic light **(Popham Rd.)**, turn **right**, cross the railroad and turn **left** onto **East Parkway**. You may wish to walk your turn here, as this is a congested area.

Follow East Parkway through downtown Scarsdale, which resembles a suburb of London more than a suburb of New York. Curve **right** onto **Crane Rd.** at the parkway entrance, then take the first **left** onto **Fox Meadow Rd**. This is a flat, wide, quiet street flanked with large homes. Continue about 4 miles straight into White Plains — the road will change names twice, first to **Walworth Ave.**, then to **Fisher Ave**.

Bear **left** onto **Bank St.**, then cross many lanes of traffic to turn **left** onto **Hamilton Ave.** Note that this area is very congested weekdays and Saturdays. Just past the railroad underpass turn right onto a road marked with a "No Outlet" sign, then turn left onto the **bike path**. This will lead you past the **County Center** parking lot (the northern end of the parkway closing zone on bicycle Sundays) and all the way to the foot of Kensico Dam. The only turn on the path is at the **North White Plains** railroad station: Do not go under the tracks, but rather turn **left**, ride through the **station parking lot**, then make a **left** at **Fisher**

Lane. The path resumes as a **right** turn just past a steel-deck bridge. You may wish to visit **Washington's Headquarters**. To do so, turn **right** where **Virginia Rd.** crosses the path.

By the time you reach **Kensico Dam**, you'll be warmed up for the only serious hill of the route — a climb up an old brick auto road to the top of the dam. Cross the busy road at the entrance to the park below the dam, make a slight right turn and proceed up this tree-lined, smooth **brick path**. At the top, turn **left** and cross the dam. Admire the view of Kensico Reservoir on your right and central Westchester on your left as you cross.

Follow the road alongside the reservoir for a mile until you reach a T by some large waterworks buildings. Turn **left** onto **Columbus Ave.**, and enjoy a speedy descent into Valhalla. Watch your speed! The hill gets steep before you know it.

Enjoy a stop at Kensico Dam Plaza, which will be on your left. Then turn **right** onto the **bike path** and return to White Plains. For those who wish a somewhat smoother ride, at the steel deck bridge **(Fisher Lane)**, turn **right**, cross the parkway, make the first **left** on **Edgepark Rd.**, and then **left** at the T onto **Kensico Rd.**, which takes you to the back of the County Center building. Here you must cross the parkway to rejoin the bike path in the County Center parking lot. Note that getting to Kensico Rd. involves a steep climb.

In White Plains, you may wish to return the way you came (cross Hamilton Ave., ride through the old bus station next to the train station, then **left** onto **Main St.**, **right** onto **Bank St.**, **right** at **Fisher Ave.**) or follow the bike path, which is unpaved in sections but always smooth and very beautiful. Cross Main St. onto the sidewalk between the northbound Bronx River Pkwy. exit ramp and the railroad. The path starts paved then will become unpaved in sections as it goes right next to the Bronx River. Use caution at several railroad and parkway underpasses — the path is often muddy (impassable if right after a flooding rain) and headroom is low. The path ends just past some tennis courts. Emerge by a church near the Hartsdale Station. Carefully walk or ride against traffic through the station parking lot, then climb to Fenimore Rd. and cross over the railroad.

BRONX RIVER VALLEY
24.0 Miles

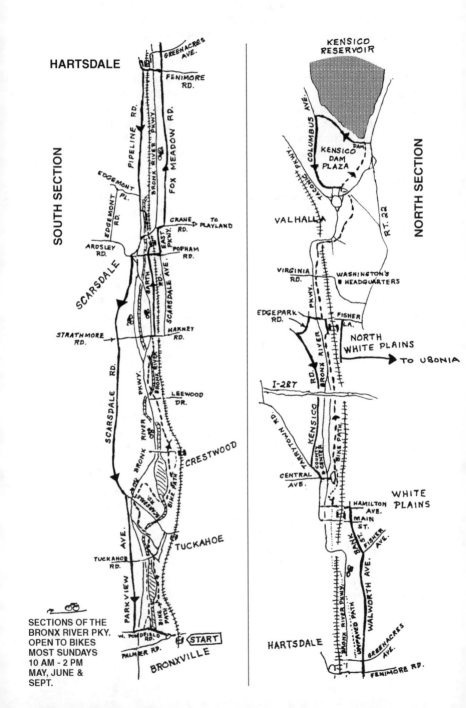

SOUTH SECTION

HARTSDALE

GREENACRES AVE.

FENIMORE RD.

PIPELINE RD.

BRONX RIVER PKWY.

FOX MEADOW RD.

EDGEMONT PL.

EDGEMONT RD.

CRANE RD.

TO PLAYLAND

ARDSLEY RD.

EAST PKWY.

POPHAM RD.

SCARSDALE

BIKE PATH

SCARSDALE AVE.

HARNEY RD.

STRATHMORE RD.

BRONX RIVER PKWY.

LEEWOOD DR.

SCARSDALE RD.

BRONX RIVER

BIKE PATH

CRESTWOOD

CRANFORD RD.

TUCKAHOE

PARKVIEW AVE.

TUCKAHOE RD.

BIKE PATH

W. POND FIELD RD.

START

PALMER RD.

BRONXVILLE

SECTIONS OF THE BRONX RIVER PKY. OPEN TO BIKES MOST SUNDAYS 10 AM - 2 PM MAY, JUNE & SEPT.

NORTH SECTION

KENSICO RESERVOIR

COLUMBUS AVE.

KENSICO DAM PLAZA

DAM

TACONIC PKWY.

RT. 22

VALHALLA

VIRGINIA RD.

WASHINGTON'S HEADQUARTERS

BRONX RIVER PKWY.

EDGEPARK RD.

FISHER LA.

NORTH WHITE PLAINS

TO USONIA

I-287

TARRYTOWN RD.

KENSICO

COUNTY CENTER

BIKE PATH

CENTRAL AVE.

WHITE PLAINS

HAMILTON AVE.

MAIN ST.

FISHER AVE.

BANK ST.

WALWORTH AVE.

BRONX RIVER PKWY.

UNPAVED PATH

HARTSDALE

GREENACRES AVE.

FENIMORE RD.

If you've skipped the path and returned on **Fisher Ave.**, which becomes **Walworth Ave.**, turn **right** at the second Hartsdale traffic light onto **Fenimore Rd**. Cross the tracks by the Hartsdale station.

Turn right into the **station plaza** (parking lot). You will notice a small road going under the overpass you were just on and paralleling the railroad: this is **Pipeline Rd.**, a straight, flat shot to Scarsdale with nothing but woods on one side and the tracks on the other. About one-quarter mile after you pass the one side street (Edgemont Pl., on right), look for **a small opening in the guardrail** on your left. Walk your bike down a path and over a **footbridge** crossing the skinny Bronx River. Turn **right** on the **path** next to the tracks, which leads you directly into the **Scarsdale station** parking lot.

At the end of the station road, turn **right** at the traffic light onto **Popham Rd**. Cross the parkway, then turn **left** onto **Scarsdale Rd.**, which forks off the southbound parkway entrance ramp. Follow Scarsdale Rd. to **Strathmore Rd.** At this point, you may either turn **left**, cross the parkway and return on the **bike path** from Harney Rd. to Pondfield Rd., or go **straight** on **Scarsdale Rd.** for several miles to **Parkview Ave**. Turn **right** on Parkview to Pondfield Rd. In either case, turn **left** on **Pondfield Rd.** to return to **Bronxville station** (end of route).

GREENWICH SAMPLER - 26.1 Miles

Terrain: Rolling, with several "shorties but steepies" (hills, that is). Very gentle terrain near the Sound (last 11 miles of route).
Traffic: Incredibly light, considering how close you are to the metropolis. A few short busy stretches, noted on the cue sheet.
Road Conditions: Superb. Greenwich has a low per-capita pothole rate.
Points of Interest: The amazing contrasts of the town of **Greenwich** — from the wealthy, woodsy **backcountry** to the New England charm of the **shoreside villages; Binney Park; The Bruce Museum; Greenwich Point** and **Byram Parks.**

It is possible to ride a good distance entirely within the boundaries of the town of Greenwich and see a sampling of the entire New England region — from woodsy, hilly interior with its stone walls, ponds and streams, to neat villages and saltwater vistas.

Start in Byram, a section of Greenwich that used to call itself East Port Chester after its busy neighbor across the Byram River. Head up pretty Pemberwick Rd. to the bustling inland settlement of Glenville. Before reaching Glenville, you might wish to look at an old mill that has been converted to shops, offices and restaurants. A particularly impressive waterfall, where the Byram River goes over the mill dam, is visible from the back of the complex.

The ride from west to east over colorfully named streets such as Clapboard Ridge Road, Dingletown Road and Cat Rock Road takes you over numerous ridges which will alternately give your low gears and brakes good workouts. Look for several very old graveyards along the way that tell of the time this was a thriving farming section.

Cross the Mianus River, then head down to Old Greenwich. This is probably the neatest of the New Englandy villages within Greenwich. Binney Park is so picture perfect that many wedding parties are photographed by the pond here, and it is a good lunch spot.

The route back heads out toward Greenwich Point, where excellent views of bay and Sound are visible from the road. Unfortunately, Greenwich Point Park, which is the nicest park on the

GREENWICH SAMPLER
26.1 Miles

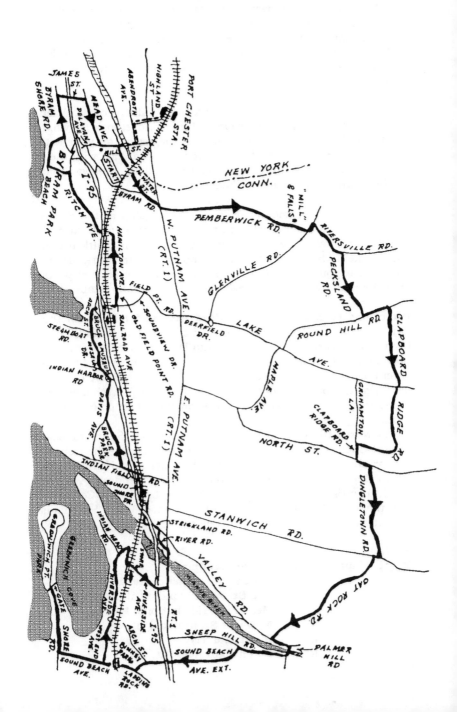

Sound, is open only to town residents. From November to March the gatehouse is empty, and during slow non-summer weekdays cyclists might be able to ask nicely to enter for a ride around. It is worth the trouble, because there are several miles of roads in the park with superb views, especially on clear days when New York is visible.

Next head through Riverside, a section of wealthy homes. After crossing the railroad on an ornate old iron bridge, look for what has to be the smallest general store in the region on your left. There is no sign out front, but the crowd of local kids with their banana-seat bikes leaning on the fence is a dead giveaway that the small white house behind the fence is a store.

Cyclists who enjoy modern art may wish to stop at the Bruce Museum, an excellent small art and science museum. Return to Byram on a road that changes names three times in a little over a mile. Take a last look at the Sound in Byram Park before returning to your car or train. If you are hungry for pizza or pasta after the ride, Byram sports several excellent Italian restaurants.

Directions to Starting Point: Mead Ave. and Mill St. in the Byram section of Greenwich is located close to Exit 2 of I-95 (the Connecticut Turnpike). Turn left onto Delavan Ave. if exiting off northbound I-95 and right if coming off southbound I-95. In several blocks you will see a firehouse on the left. Mead Ave. is the left turn just past the firehouse, and Delavan Ave. changes its name to Mill St. at this point. Park on the street or in nearby municipal parking lots.

Metro-North Directions: Take a New Haven Line Stamford local to Port Chester. Carry your bikes down the stairs at the front of the platform, then ride away from the tracks on Highland St. Cross Main St. (Rt. 1), then take the next left (Abendroth Ave.). At the T, turn right onto Mill St. Cross the little bridge into Connecticut, then turn left at the traffic light onto North Water St. This is the intersection at Mile 0.1 of the cue sheet.

Pt. to Point	Cume	Turn	Street/Landmark
0.0	0.0	L	Start at the corner of **Mead Ave. and Mill St**. While standing at the end of Mead Ave., ride **left** onto **Mill St.**
0.1	0.1	R	**N. Water St.** (traffic light)
0.5	0.6	L	**Byram Rd.** (T)
0.2	0.8	R	**W. Putnam Ave. (Rt. 1)** (T)

Pt. to Point	Cume	Turn	Street/Landmark
0.0	0.8	L	Get in the left turn lane immediately and turn into **Pemberwick Rd.**
1.9	2.7		Old mill and falls on left
0.1	2.8	L	**Glenville Rd.** (T)
0.1	2.9	R	**Riversville Rd.** (traffic light)
0.5	3.4	R	**Pecksland Rd.**
1.5	4.9	L	**Round Hill Rd.** (T)
0.7	5.6	R	**Clapboard Ridge Rd.**
0.9	6.5	R	**Lake Ave.** (T)
0.0	6.5	L	Immediate **left** to continue on **Clapboard Ridge Rd.**
1.1	7.6	L	At T and stop sign to continue on **Clapboard Ridge Rd.** (Grahamton Lane goes left)
0.3	7.9	L	**North St.** (T)
0.2	8.1	R	**Dingletown Rd.**
1.3	9.4	R	**Stanwich Rd.** (T)
0.1	9.5	L	Immediate **left** onto **Cat Rock Rd.**
1.9	11.4	L	**Valley Rd.** (T)
0.2	11.6	R	**Palmer Hill Rd.**
0.1	11.7	R	**Sheephill Rd.** (first right after bridge over Mianus River)
0.7	12.4	L	**Sound Beach Ave. Extension**
0.5	12.9	S	Cross E. Putnam Ave. (Rt. 1)
0.5	13.4	BR	At little rotary to continue on **Sound Beach Ave**. Laddins Rock Rd. goes left. **Binney Park** will be on your right after turning
1.3	14.7	R	**Shore Rd.** (T)
0.8	15.5		Entrance to Greenwich Point Park. Cycle back the way you came
0.8	16.3	L	**Sound Beach Ave.**
0.9	17.2	L	**West End Ave.** (traffic light)
0.3	17.5	L	At little rotary onto **Riverside Ave.**
0.8	18.3	BR	At fork to continue on **Riverside Ave.** Indian Head Rd. goes left (no sign)
0.5	18.8	L	At stop sign to continue on **Riverside Ave**. Cross old iron overpass over rail road tracks. (Oval Ave. goes right)
0.1	18.9		Store disguised as small white house on your left shortly after crossing the tracks
0.5	19.4	L	**Rt. 1** (traffic light). CAUTION: Busy road
0.3	19.7	L	**River Rd.** (next traffic light. CAUTION:

Pt. to Point	Cume	Turn	Street/Landmark
			Go to right side of road then walk or ride across Rt. 1 when light changes; do not attempt to bike the turn from the left lane)
0.7	20.4	L	**Strickland Ave.** (Cos Cob Historical Society directly in front of you at this turn. Turn **right** at this corner if you wish to view more old Cos Cob homes)
0.3	20.7	L	**Sound Shore Dr.** (street goes under railroad immediately)
0.4	21.1	L	**Indian Field Rd.** (traffic light). Cross over I-95 after turn
0.3	21.4	R	**Bruce Park Dr.**
0.5	21.9	R	Road becomes **Davis Ave.** at curve in road near pond (on left)
0.3	22.2	S	At circle. Road changes name to **Indian Harbor Rd.**
0.1	22.3	R	**Museum Dr.** (Bruce Museum will be on the right)
0.2	22.5	S	Cross Steamboat Rd. at traffic light. Road becomes **Arch St.** and goes under I-95 and railroad. CAUTION: Traffic is heavy around Turnpike entrances. Obey red lights!
0.3	22.8	L	**Railroad Ave.** (traffic light beyond railroad underpass). Road will change name to **Old Field Point Rd., Hamilton Ave.** and **Ritch Ave.** as you ride along
1.4	24.2	L	Into **Byram Park**
0.1	24.3	R	After passing entrance booth. Ride past a small marina
0.3	24.6	L	**Byram Shore Rd.** (T)
1.0	25.6	R	**James St.**
0.2	25.8	R	**Mead Ave.** (T)
0.3	26.1		Return to **Mill St. and Mead Ave.** (end of route)

GREENWICH-ARMONK - 36.2 MILES

Terrain: Rolling with quite a few short but intensely steep stretches.
Traffic: For the most part, incredibly light. They don't call the northern part of Greenwich "the back country" for nothing.
Road Conditions: Excellent. One small stretch of dirt road.
Points of Interest: The immense wealth and beauty of **Back Country Greenwich**; **outdoor sculpture garden** at Pepsico; **SUNY/Purchase** campus; **Westchester Airport**; park in Armonk for picnics; **Audubon Center** of Greenwich.

Greenwich is an immense town stretching ten miles inland from Long Island Sound. The interior section contains miles of quiet, well-paved roads which pass large estates set amongst woods and fields. Don't be surprised if deer bound across your path.

Start in Byram, Greenwich's only true "working class" district. After following the Byram River inland for two miles, turn left into New York State. At the top of a very steep hill is a large castle that formerly housed the Museum of Cartoon Art before Beetle Bailey creator Mort Walker moved it to Florida.

Next head to Pepsico World Headquarters. Their fine outdoor sculpture collection is open to the public. Across the road is the campus of the State University of New York at Purchase. This school is known for its theater and dance curriculum. A broad, sunny brick plaza is located above the tunnel that you cycle through.

Continue north on King St., the road that forms the border between New York and Connecticut. You may wish to take a side trip to Westchester Airport, a very busy facility that still retains its small-airport look (you can watch planes take off with your nose pressed against a fence at field level).

Slice through a corner of Connecticut before re-emerging in New York. Have lunch in the pleasant town of Armonk, which has several delicatessens and a nice park, complete with gaggles of Canada geese.

GREENWICH-ARMONK
36.2 Miles

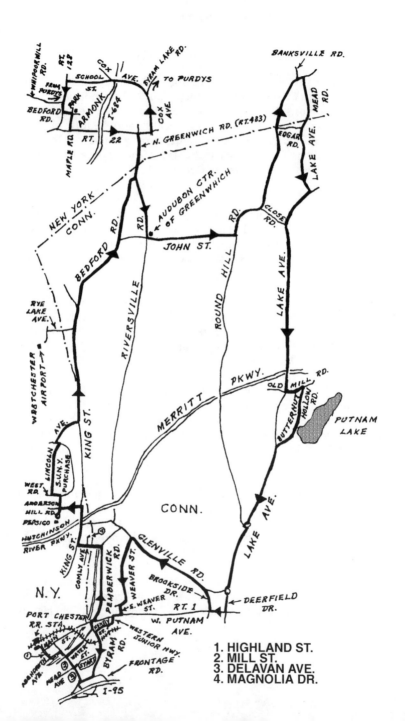

1. HIGHLAND ST.
2. MILL ST.
3. DELAVAN AVE.
4. MAGNOLIA DR.

Then turn south toward the Sound. On the way back you will pass the Audubon Center (an interesting hiking area) and a house on Brookside Dr. that is as big as any palace.

Directions to Starting Point: Mead Ave. and Mill St. in the Byram section of Greenwich is located close to Exit 2 of I-95 (the Connecticut Turnpike). Turn left onto Delavan Ave. if exiting off northbound I-95 and right if coming off southbound I-95. In several blocks you will see a firehouse on the left. Mead Ave. is the left turn just past the firehouse, and Delavan Ave. changes its name to Mill St. at this point. Park on the street or in nearby municipal parking lots.

Metro-North Directions: Take a New Haven Line Stamford local to Port Chester. Carry your bikes down the stairs at the front of the platform, then ride away from the tracks on Highland St. Cross Main St. (Rt. 1), then take the next left (Abendroth Ave.). At the T, turn right onto Mill St. Cross the little bridge into Connecticut, then turn left at the traffic light onto North Water St. This is the intersection at Mile 0.1 of the cue sheet.

Note: You may combine this route with the Armonk-Purdys route (page 65) to make a challenging 82.1-mile ride. At the fork at Mile 13.0, bear right onto Byram Rd. (no sign). Pick up the Armonk-Purdys route at Mile 1.5, then, at the end of the Armonk-Purdys route (the intersection of Rt. 128 and Bedford Rd.), return to the Greenwich-Armonk route at Mile 14.6.

Pt. to Point	Cume	Turn	Street/Landmark
0.0	0.0	L	Start at the corner of **Mead Ave. and Mill St**. While standing at the end of Mead Ave., ride **left** onto **Mill St.**
0.1	0.1	R	**N. Water St.** (traffic light)
0.5	0.6	L	**Byram Rd.** (T)
0.1	0.7	R	**W. Putnam Ave.** (Rt. 1) (T)
0.1	0.8	L	Get in left turn lane immediately and turn into **Pemberwick Rd.**
1.2	2.0	L	**Comly Ave.** (possibly no sign). Street crosses over concrete bridge, then ascends steep hill
0.3	2.3		Large house on right at Magnolia Dr. was site of Museum of Cartoon Art
0.2	2.5	R	**King St.** (T)
1.7	4.2	L	**Anderson Hill Rd.** (blinking yellow light)
0.9	5.1	L	Into **Pepsico Headquarters** at traffic light

Pt. to Point	Cume	Turn	Street/Landmark
0.3	5.4		Outdoor sculpture garden
			U-turn and return the way you came
0.3	5.7	S	At traffic light into **SUNY/Purchase** campus
0.1	5.8	L	**West Rd.** (T)
0.1	5.9	R	**Lincoln Ave.** (through campus)
1.1	7.0	L	At stop sign (no street sign)
0.0	7.0	R	Immediate **right** onto street with open gate. You will pass maintenance garage on your right
0.6	7.6	L	**King St.** (stop sign)
1.2	8.8		Turn **left** at Rye Lake Ave. (traffic light) for side trip to **Westchester Airport**
0.5	9.3	R	**Bedford Rd.**
2.6	11.9	L	**Riversville Rd.** (T). Proceed into New York State
0.8	12.7	R	**Rt. 22** (traffic light)
0.1	12.8	L	**Cox Ave.** (blinking light)
0.2	13.0	BL	At fork to continue on **Cox Ave.** *(Bear right here to join Armonk-Purdys route)*
0.7	13.7	BL	At fork by cemetery after crossing I-684 to go onto **School St.** (Cox Ave. goes right)
0.3	14.0	L	**Rt. 128** (T)
0.5	14.5		Delicatessens available in the center of **Armonk**
0.1	14.6	L	**Bedford Rd.** (blinking light) *(Return from Armonk-Purdys route)*
0.2	14.8	R	**Maple Ave.** (stop sign and red blinking light; picnic **park** is located diagonally across the street at this corner)
0.1	14.9	L	**Rt. 22** (traffic light)
0.7	15.6	R	**N. Greenwich Rd. (Rt. 433)** (traffic light). Road becomes **Riversville Rd.** when you re-enter Connecticut
0.8	16.4	BL	To continue on **Riversville Rd.** (Bedford Rd. goes right)
1.4	17.8	L	**John St. (Audubon Center of Greenwich** on left)
1.4	19.2	L	**Round Hill Rd.** (T)
0.8	20.0	BL	To continue on **Round Hill Rd.** (Close Rd. goes right)
2.0	22.0	S	At stop sign (Banksville Rd. goes left)

Pt. to Point	Cume	Turn	Street/Landmark
0.0	22.0	R	Immediate **right** onto **Mead Rd.**
0.4	22.4		Becomes dirt road. Pavement resumes shortly
0.3	22.7	BL	Onto **Lake Ave.** (Edgar Rd. goes right)
0.7	23.4	R	To continue on **Lake Ave.** (stop sign)
0.7	24.1	BL	To continue on **Lake Ave.** (Close Rd. goes right)
1.9	26.0	L	**Old Mill Rd.** (no sign) at stop sign after crossing Merritt Pkwy.
0.2	26.2	R	**Butternut Hollow Rd.** (yield sign)
0.9	27.1	L	**Lake Ave.** (T)
2.1	29.2	S	At rotary to continue on **Lake Ave.** (Round Hill Rd. goes right)
1.2	30.4	S	Go halfway around rotary toward Greenwich Business District and onto **Dearfield Dr.**
0.4	30.8	R	**Rt. 1** (traffic light)
0.1	30.9	R	**Brookside Dr.** (next traffic light). Look for huge house on the left
0.5	31.4	BL	**Glenville Rd.** (T)
1.6	33.0	L	**Weaver St.** (by Texaco station)
1.6	34.6	L	**E. Weaver St.** just past Greenwich Office Park
0.1	34.7	R	**W. Putnam Ave. (Rt. 1)**
0.2	34.9	L	**Western Junior Highway** (next traffic light)
0.3	35.2	R	**Henry St.**
0.2	35.4	BL	At top of sudden rise to continue on **Henry St.**
0.0	35.4	L	**Byram Ave.** (stop sign; no street sign)
0.4	35.8	R	**Frontage Rd.** (T)
0.1	35.9	R	**Delavan Ave.** (traffic light)
0.3	36.2	L	Return to **Mead Ave. and Mill St.** (end of route)

RIDES STARTING IN CENTRAL WESTCHESTER

Central Westchester is not as well known as other parts of the county for good cycling because of its busy roads, but this guidebook will steer you to great places to cycle not too far from the bustling county seat of White Plains.

Although these routes do not have majestic bodies of water such as Long Island Sound or the Hudson River to ride next to (although two rides do feature views of the Hudson), there are other attractive parts of Westchester geography featured — deep, somewhat hilly woods of areas north of Westchester Airport and the quiet woods surrounding the Kensico and New Croton reservoirs, for example. There is also much history in Sleepy Hollow Country, and the tranquility of Rockefeller country near Pocantico Hills takes the cyclist back to a quieter time.

The North County Trailway, featured in two of the rides in this section, is an ambitious project of Westchester County and New York State to turn an entire 30-plus former railroad right-of-way from the Bronx to the Putnam County line into a paved bike path. It is shear pleasure to ride the smooth path without fear of cars.

Sleepy Hollow Special specializes in the landmarks of the land of Washington Irving, creator of Rip Van Winkle and Ichabod Crane. Tour Irving's Sunnyside mansion and the nearby Lyndhurst castle (the two are connected by a ride atop the New York City aqueduct). Then head to Phillipsburg Manor's working mill and colonial farm life exhibitions. Sleepy Hollow Cemetery and the Old Dutch Church are next, followed by Rockwood Hall, a delightful place to have a picnic (unfortunately, bicycles are not allowed on the grounds, so lock them at the entrance and walk in). Return through the rolling quiet of Pocantico Hills. A new spur of this route lets the cyclist enjoy a section of the North County Trailway.

North White Plains-Usonia, half of the White Plains-Bedford route of the former edition of this *RIDE GUIDE*, circles Kensico Reservoir, tours Pepsico's outdoor sculpture garden and SUNY/ Purchase and then heads for Usonia, a beautiful woodsy neighborhood of homes designed by Frank Lloyd Wright.

Westchester Airport-Bedford, the other half of the White Plains-Bedford route, follows the old "Dan Henry" route of quiet, hilly backroads in Greenwich's back country before ending at the New Englandy town green of Bedford.

North County Trailway features a good chunk of the former Putnam branch of the New York Central, now a smooth bikeway. At the shores of the New Croton Reservoir, head west to hug the shore of the waterway, including several miles of hard-packed quiet dirt road where the only cars belong to fishermen. Some stunning Hudson River views are available in Scarborough before heading through Pocantico Hills enroute to the finish at Briarcliff.

SLEEPY HOLLOW SPECIAL - 24.4 or 30.0 MILES

Terrain: Hilly, with a few memorable climbs. But some parts of the route, notably on the North County Trailway and in Philipse Manor, aren't too bad!

Traffic: Fairly light, except one short run on Rt. 119 and two short stretches on Rt. 9 which are busy. No traffic at all on the North County Trailway.

Road Conditions: Mostly good. The short stretch of aqueduct riding is unpaved.

Points of Interest: Two **Sleepy Hollow Restorations; Sunnyside** (Washington Irving's home) and **Philipsburg Manor**; the **Lyndhurst Mansion; Sleepy Hollow Cemetery** and **Old Dutch Church; Rockwood Hall** (site of former Rockefeller mansion on Hudson, now a beautiful grassy area to have a picnic); scenic roads and homes in **Philipse Manor** and **Pocantico Hills**; sections of **North County Trailway**, including one by pretty **Tarrytown Lakes**.

Many of **Central Westchester's** finest historic and scenic areas are incorporated in this route. The terrain makes it necessary to put a little effort into the cycling here, but most of the steeper climbs are short and on quiet roads that allow walking if necessary without interfering with auto traffic.

Ride by the lovely Tarrytown Lakes on a new section of the North County Trailway, with the towers of Marymount College in the distance. Then climb through the hilly campus before eventually emerging onto Westchester's "corporate strip," Rt. 119.

Head down toward the Hudson on Taxter Rd. The killer climb away from Rt. 119 is rewarded by a steady hill into Irvington.

Sunnyside, at the bottom of another nice hill, was the home of Washington Irving, the 19th-century author whose books include characters such as Rip Van Winkle and Ichabod Crane. This is one of three restored homes run by Sleepy Hollow Restorations. You may purchase a joint ticket and visit all three. This tour passes two sites and the third, Van Cortlandt Manor, is on the two Croton routes (pages 74 and 78), and only a 20-minute car drive north. The tours at these restored homes are excellent; they are given by informative hosts and hostesses in period costumes.

After visiting Sunnyside, ride atop the New York City aqueduct to

Lyndhurst. This 19th-century mansion requires a separate admission fee.

Head to Tarrytown next. Ride through this busy village on quiet side roads paralleling Rt. 9. Two more historic sites are located across the road from each other in North Tarrytown: Philipsburg Manor, with its working waterwheel and picturesque mill pond, and Sleepy Hollow Cemetery. The ride around the cemetery is 1.7 miles and quite beautiful, especially the road next to the Pocantico River. Be sure to stop and see the Old Dutch Church. You may wish to look for Washington Irving's grave.

The route next enters the pretty, wealthy residential section along the Hudson River called Philipse Manor. Cyclists coming by train start the route here. Next, ride by Phelps Hospital to get to Rockwood Hall. There used to be a mansion here owned by the Rockefeller Family. The house is gone but the beautiful lawn on a hillside overlooking the river has been open to the public as a recreation spot. For many years mountain bikes were allowed at Rockwood Hall but the area has just been closed to ATBers. Lock your bike near the entrance, walk in and enjoy a picnic.

The final 10 miles of the route goes through Pocantico Hills, an anomaly in busy central Westchester. The reason why this section contains woods, fields, a working cattle farm and a picture-perfect village rather than houses, factories and office buildings is that most of the land is owned by the Rockefeller family. A good part of the estate has been donated to the New York State park system and is open to the public for hiking and horseback riding, but not off-road cycling.

Upon return to the car starting point, you may wish to ride an extra 5.6-mile round-trip sprint on a dead-end spur of the North County Trailway, a quiet wooded section of the path paralleling some busy highways, but without the traffic, of course!

Directions to the Starting Point: The Eastview Park and Ride Lot is on Saw Mill River Rd., just west of the Saw Mill River Pkwy. Eastview exit (which is the first exit coming north from I-287 eastbound). If you are coming from White Plains on I-287 westbound, exit at the Sprain Brook Pkwy. north, turn off at Rt. 100C. Turn left on 100C, which runs into Saw Mill River Rd. near the former Union Carbide offices. (If the Park and Ride Lot is full, continue to Marymount College, where street parking is available).

SLEEPY HOLLOW SPECIAL
24.4 or 30.0 Miles

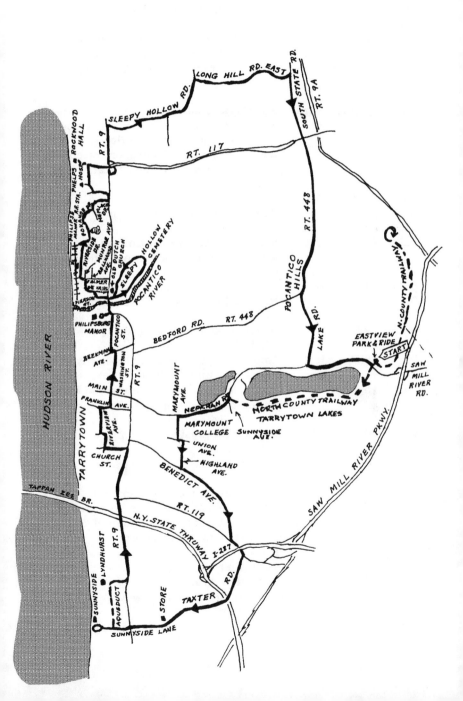

Metro-North Directions: Take a Hudson Line local train to
Philipse Manor. Walk your bike onto the road adjacent to the
platform, then ride north (the river and the tracks will be on your
left). You are now on Riverside Dr., heading toward the turn at
Mile 12.8. When you reach the end of the cue sheet, cycle back
to the train station by following the route from the beginning.

Pt. to Point	Cume	Turn	Street/Landmark
0.0	0.0	S	Exit Eastview Park and Ride and cross Saw Mill River Rd. to enter **North County Trailway**. Climb short, steep hill toward water house at end of Tarrytown Lakes
0.8	0.8	S	Cross unmarked road
0.3	1.1	L	**Neperan Rd**. Do not go left on Sunnyside Ave.
0.2	1.3	L	At sign for **Marymount College** onto **Marymount Ave.** Ride through the campus
0.3	1.6	L	**Union Ave.** (stop sign)
0.1	1.7	R	**Highland Ave.** (stop sign; the street sign is on the left)
0.3	2.0	L	**Benedict Ave.** (traffic light)
1.0	3.0	L	**Rt. 119** (T)
0.5	3.5	R	**Taxter Rd.** (traffic light immediately after riding under I-287)
1.6	5.1		Road changes name to **Sunnyside Lane**; Brookside Deli on right
0.6	5.7	S	At traffic light (cross Rt. 9)
0.4	6.1	BR	To enter **Sunnyside**, Washington Irving's home
0.2	6.3		**U-turn** and head back the way you came in
0.3	6.6	L	**Bike Route** (aqueduct; unpaved)
0.6	7.2		Enter **Lyndhurst Mansion** grounds. Ride directly out to Rt. 9 (right) if you do not wish to tour the mansion
0.2	7.4	L	**Rt. 9**
1.3	8.7	L	**Church St.**
0.1	8.8	R	**Riverview Ave.**
0.1	8.9	R	To continue on **Riverview Ave.** (Bridge St. goes straight)
0.1	9.0	BL	To continue on **Riverview Ave.** (no sign)

Pt. to Point	Cume	Turn	Street/Landmark
0.1	9.1	R	At stop sign (no street sign) onto **Franklin Ave.**
0.1	9.2	L	First left (no street sign) onto **Washington St.**
0.7	9.9	L	**Beekman Ave.**
0.1	10.0	R	**Pocantico St.**
0.3	10.3	SL	**Sharp left** at light to enter **Philipsburg Manor -- Upper Mills**; after touring Manor, turn **left** onto **Rt. 9 North**
0.1	10.4	R	Into gate of **Sleepy Hollow Cemetery. Old Dutch Church of Sleepy Hollow** is on your left as you enter. Ride around the perimeter of the cemetery, first following the brook (which is on your right)
1.7	12.1	S	Exit the cemetery through the entrance you came in. Go **straight** across Rt. 9 onto **Pierson St.**, which changes name to **Bellwood Ave.**
0.2	12.3	L	**DeVries Ave.**
0.1	12.4	R	**Munroe Ave.**
0.1	12.5	L	**Palmer Ave.** (stop sign)
0.1	12.6	R	Curve right toward **Philipse Manor train station**
0.2	12.8	BL	At fork onto **Riverside Dr.**, which changes name to **Pokahoe Dr.**
0.9	13.7	L	**Hemlock Dr.** (T)
0.3	14.0	L	**Rt. 9 North** (T)
0.1	14.1	L	Turn **left** immediately at traffic light toward **Phelps Memorial Hospital Center**
0.1	14.2	BR	Toward main entrance of hospital
0.2	14.4	R	After passing hospital's main entrance
0.1	14.5		**Rockwood Hall** entrance on left through barricade (no bicycling on grounds). IBM entrance is straight ahead
0.3	14.8	R	Toward Rts. 9 and 117 (if you are coming out of Rockwood Hall, this will be straight)
0.3	15.1	R	Toward **Rt. 9**
0.1	15.2	R	**Rt. 9 North**
1.1	16.3	R	**Sleepy Hollow Rd.**
1.3	17.6	BL	At fork (no street sign)

Pt. to Point	Cume	Turn	Street/Landmark
1.3	18.9	R	**Long Hill Rd. East**. CAUTION: In 0.6 miles, road becomes steep and curvy — control your speed!
1.1	20.0	R	**South State Rd.** (T)
0.8	20.8	S	**Rt. 448** (traffic light; cross Rt. 117)
2.4	23.2	BL	At fork by Pocantico Hills green onto **Lake Rd.**
0.7	23.9	L	At T and stop sign with Tarrytown Lakes in front of you; no street sign
0.5	24.4	L	Into **Eastview Park and Ride Lot**. You can end route here, or continue onto the North County Trailway spur headed north
0.0	24.4	R	Immediate **right** onto **North County Trailway** (parallels road then curves left up short, steep hill)
0.1	24.5	L	At junction of two paths
2.7	27.2		**U turn** at end of paved trail
2.7	29.9	BR	At trail fork. Do not go over Saw Mill Pkwy.
0.1	30.0		**Eastview Park and Ride Lot**. End of route

NORTH WHITE PLAINS — USONIA - 25.1 MILES

Terrain: Quite hilly, as this is the heart of hilly interior Westchester. But no real killer hills -- you'll warm up to the terrain changes!
Traffic: Light to moderate, with a few busy roads.
Road Conditions: Pretty good, except for Hall Ave. and Buckout Road, which are rough and full of potholes.
Points of Interest: campuses of **Manhattanville College** and **SUNY/Purchase; Westchester County Airport; Frank Lloyd Wright** homes in **Usonia**; riding over **Kensico Dam.**

Ride through the heart of interior Westchester on this somewhat challenging route. The end of this ride incorporates part of the White Plains-Bedford route from the first edition of *RIDE GUIDE/Hudson Valley and Sound Shore*, a very challenging course that has been split into two rides for this edition.

Start by heading through the backwoods section near White Plains represented by Buckout Road, a hilly and winding course. This area used to be somewhat "hick" complete with small cottages and shack-like dwellings, but the houses now are decidedly upscale and becoming more frequent. There is a nice view as you exit this part of the route.

Then head toward Manhattanville College, a pretty campus that includes an old castle. For contrasting architecture, cycle through SUNY/Purchase, the state university specializing in the arts and dance.

Next stop is Westchester Airport, a busy facility that still retains its "small-town" feel. Lock your bike up and have a snack in the terminal.

The final part of the route circles Kensico Reservoir, starting with Usonia, the wooded area of homes designed by Frank Lloyd Wright. Ascend to the Kensico Dam, and cross over the dam, with its beautiful view of reservoir to the left and the area you pedaled through on the right. Descend from the dam on an old brick auto road, then take the Bronx River Pkwy. bike path back to North White Plains.
Directions to the Starting Point: The North White Plains Railroad Station is located off the Bronx River Pkwy. at Fisher

NORTH WHITE PLAINS-USONIA
25.1 Miles

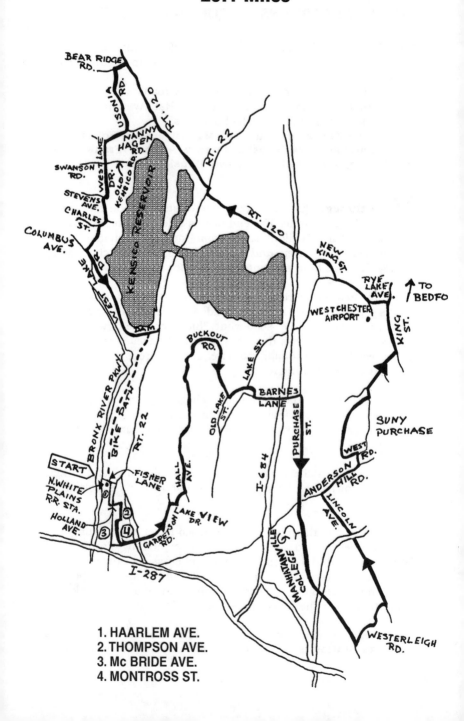

1. HAARLEM AVE.
2. THOMPSON AVE.
3. Mc BRIDE AVE.
4. MONTROSS ST.

Lane (right turn off northbound parkway). There is a fee for parking here. On Bicycle Sundays in May, June and September, the parkway is closed between 10-2. Plan to arrive before the closing or take the Sprain Brook Pkwy. to Rt. 100C, turn right, go straight onto Rt. 100 south, then in about a mile turn left onto Virginia Rd. Turn right (south) at the Bronx River Pkwy., then turn left at Fisher Lane to the station.

Metro-North Directions: Take a Harlem Line train local or express to North White Plains. Go downstairs to the main parking lot, where the route begins.

Note: You can combine this route with the Bronx River Valley route (page 23), which is especially convenient on Bicycle Sundays. You can also combine this ride with Westchester Airport-Bedford (page 52), for a 59.9-mile challenge.

Pt. to Point	Cume	Turn	Street/Landmark
0.0	0.0	R	Exit North White Plains railroad station parking lot at fee collector's booth (north end) and turn **right** onto **Fisher Lane**. Carefully ride through one-lane railroad underpass
0.0	0.0	R	**Haarlem Ave.** (ride through to end; at Do Not Enter, walk bike one block against traffic)
0.3	0.3	L	**Holland Ave.**
0.0	0.3	S	Cross N. Broadway (Rt. 22) at traffic light
0.2	0.5	R	**Thompson Ave.**
0.1	0.6	R	**McBride Ave.**
0.1	0.7	L	**Montross St.**
0.1	0.8	L	**Orchard St.** (stop sign). Do not head toward I-287 but cross over Central Westchester Pkwy.
0.1	0.9	S	Road changes name to **Garretson Rd.** at stop sign
0.2	1.1	R	**Lake View Dr.**
0.2	1.3	L	**Hall Ave.** (T)
0.6	1.9	R	**Curve right** at large right arrow onto **Buckout Rd.** (hilly and winding; view on left near end)
1.2	3.1	L	At fork onto **Old Lake St.** (stop sign)
0.2	3.3	R	**Barnes Lane** (no street sign! Turn is first right turn on steep downhill.)
0.0	3.3	S	Cross Lake St. at stop sign. No street signs

Pt. to Point	Cume	Turn	Street/Landmark
0.0	3.3	L	At T onto **Barnes Lane**. Go over I-684
0.9	4.2	R	**Purchase St. (Rt. 120)** (T)
1.6	5.8	R	**Manhattanville College** entrance
0.0	5.8	R	Past guardhouse. Climb hill
0.2	6.0		**U-turn** at **castle** and church with modern spire; return to entrance you rode in
0.2	6.2	R	**Purchase St. (Rt. 120)**
0.4	6.6	L	**Westerleigh Rd.** (turn is just after right fork prior to traffic light at I-287)
0.8	7.4	L	**Lincoln Ave.** (T)
1.3	8.7	R	**Anderson Hill Rd.** (T; traffic light). Hot dog wagon on left
0.1	8.8	L	Into **SUNY/Purchase** at traffic light (Pepsico headquarters on right)
0.1	8.9	L	**West Rd.** (T)
0.1	9.0	R	**Lincoln Ave.** (through campus)
1.1	10.1	L	At stop sign (no street sign)
0.0	10.1	R	Immediate **right** onto street with open gate. You will pass maintenance garage on your right
0.6	10.7	L	**King St.** (stop sign)
1.2	11.9	L	**Rye Lake Ave.** (traffic light). *Riders to Bedford, go straight here and look for Cliffdale Ave. on right, which is the turn at Mile 0.3 of the Westchester Airport - Bedford route (page 54)*
0.2	12.1		**Westchester Airport**. Go **left** to enter airport and use facilities of terminal (restrooms; food) and for best view of planes. Then return to this intersection (by Gulf Station) and go **straight** on main airport exit road, toward I-684. If you are skipping the airport stop, make a **right** on main airport exit road, toward I-684
0.7	12.8	R	**New King St.**
0.3	13.1	R	**Rt. 120 North**
1.6	14.7	S	At junction of Rt. 22 to continue on **Rt. 120 North**
0.4	15.1	L	At traffic light to continue on **Rt. 120 North**
1.9	17.0	L	**Bear Ridge Rd.**

Pt. to Point	Cume	Turn	Street/Landmark
0.1	17.1	L	**Usonia Rd.** (Frank Lloyd Wright homes)
0.9	18.0	R	**Nanny Hagen Rd.** (T)
1.2	19.2	L	**West Lake Dr.** (first left turn after "hill" sign)
0.3	19.5	S	At stop sign, crossing Swanson Rd. and Old Kensico Rd.
1.3	20.8	L	To continue on **West Lake Dr.** (Stevens Ave. goes straight)
0.2	21.0	R	To continue on **West Lake Dr.** (Lockland Ave. goes left)
0.1	21.1	L	To continue on **West Lake Dr.** (Charles St. goes straight)
1.0	22.1	L	**Columbus Ave.** (T)
0.1	22.2	L	**West Lake Dr.**
0.8	23.0		Cross dam
0.5	23.5	R	Onto **brick road** (starts just past the second dam pillar)
0.4	23.9	S	Cross busy road onto paved **bike path**, which goes left to parallel road under an underpass, and then turns sharply right after the underpass toward the Bronx River Pkwy.
1.2	25.1	L	**Fisher Lane** (T). Cross steel deck bridge
0.0	25.1	R	Immediate **right** into **North White Plains Railroad Station Parking Lot**. End of route

WESTCHESTER AIRPORT- BEDFORD - 34.8 MILES

Terrain: Hilly throughout. Short, steep "roller coasters" near the beginning, followed by long ascents and descents.
Traffic: Amazingly light. You will feel you are hundreds of miles from the metropolis, rather than right around the corner from White Plains.
Road Conditions: Excellent. One stretch of dirt road near Bedford Village (the cue sheet presents a paved alternate).
Points of Interest: Backcountry Greenwich (large homes in the woods); **Bedford Village** historic district and town green; **Mianus River Gorge** hiking spot.

This is the northern part of the White Plains-Bedford tour presented in the first edition of *RIDE GUIDE Hudson Valley*. Way back in the 1970s, when the author was a teenager, this route was marked by arrows drawn by one of the great figures of cycle-touring of the era, Dan Henry. That Dan knew how to pick a great bike route, complete with ultra-quiet back roads, mile after mile of woods and streams and a destination village as picture-postcard perfect as any in New England. But better bring your hill-climbing quads and low, low, low granny gears — there are some steep climbs here!

Start at Westchester Airport, a busy field with the small-town touch. Restaurant and bathroom facilities are available in the terminal. If you wish to avoid the parking fee, there are several office complexes nearby with large parking lots.

Immediately cycle across the state line into Greenwich, Connecticut. This part of the ride features roller-coaster hills — short, steep and curvy. As you head north toward Banksville (where you re-enter New York), the hills get longer and less steep. The houses are set well back from the roads and are valued in the seven digits.

Relax on the Bedford Village green and walk around the historic town. Peek into the window of the 18th century courthouse, which recalls the days when this village and White Plains were both county seats. The New Englandy look of Bedford Village is genuine, for this area was once part of Connecticut.

Those who don't mind a steep unpaved downhill can take Miller's

WESTCHESTER AIRPORT-BEDFORD
34.8 Miles

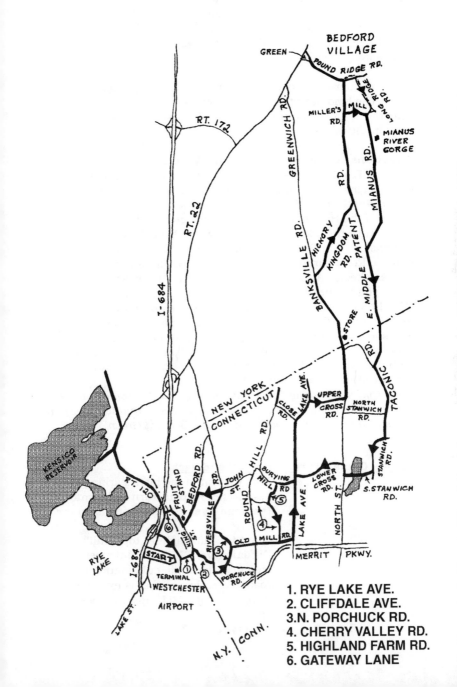

1. RYE LAKE AVE.
2. CLIFFDALE AVE.
3. N. PORCHUCK RD.
4. CHERRY VALLEY RD.
5. HIGHLAND FARM RD.
6. GATEWAY LANE

Mill Road from the top; others may opt for the bypass. Both routes meet at the scenic mill, now a private home. Stop by the Mianus River Gorge for the excellent water, which you pump yourself. Cyclists with time and energy should hike the trails here (no off-road cycling allowed) — it is a beautiful wild area with an impressively deep gorge.

Next, head back into Connecticut (the border is near a horse farm). The landmark that marks re-entry into New York, and very near the end of the route, is Purdy's fruit stand, which has good cider in the fall.

Directions to the Starting Point: Westchester Airport is located off Exit 2 of I-684. Proceed straight to main parking lot. The route begins at the parking lot exit. There is a fee for parking.

Metro-North Directions: The closest train station is North White Plains of the Harlem Division (7.7 extra miles out, 6.2 extra miles back). Take the bike path paralleling the Bronx River Pkwy. north to Kensico Dam Plaza, follow signs to Rt. 22 North, ride next to Kensico Reservoir for 3 miles to Rt. 120 South, and pedal 2 miles to Westchester Airport entrance (a left turn). An additional mile takes you to the start of the route. On the return, turn right at Mile 33.3 on Rt. 120 North and reverse the above route to return to the station. Or, for a 12-mile run each way, you can follow the cue sheet of North White Plains-Usonia to Mile 11.9, then continue straight on King Street instead of turning into the airport (although you could visit the airport to use the facilities!). Pick up the cue sheet of this route at Mile 0.3.

Note: Cyclists wishing longer routes may link this route with North White Plains-Usonia (as described above), and/or Bedford-Ridgefield (page 70), which starts at the Bedford Green.

Pt. to Point	Cume	Turn	Street/Landmark
0.0	0.0	R	From the exit to the main parking lot of Westchester Airport, turn **right** onto **Rye Lake Ave**. A Gulf station is on the left
0.2	0.2	L	**King St.** (traffic light at top of hill)
0.1	0.3	R	**Cliffdale Ave.** CAUTION: Intensely steep and curvy downhill, culminating in wood-floored bridge that is *extremely slippery when wet!* Keep your speed in check!
1.2	1.5	R	**Riversville Rd.** (T)

Pt. to Point	Cume	Turn	Street/Landmark
0.4	1.9	L	**Porchuck Rd.**
0.7	2.6	L	**N. Porchuck Rd.**
0.6	3.2	R	**Old Mill Rd.**
0.8	4.0	S	Cross Round Hill Rd. at stop sign. Store on right at intersection
1.1	5.1	L	**Lake Ave.** (T)
1.5	6.6	BR	At fork to continue on **Lake Ave.** (Close Rd. goes left)
0.6	7.2	R	**Upper Cross Rd.**
1.0	8.2	L	**North St.** (T)
1.0	9.2		Store on right at New York State border
2.0	11.2	R	**Hickory Kingdom Rd.**
1.9	13.1	BL	**E. Middle Patent Rd.**
2.2	15.3	L	**Pound Ridge Rd.** (T)
0.5	15.8	BR	At **Bedford Green** (toward Rt. 22 North)
0.1	15.9		**U-turn** at Rt. 22 and return the way you came. Stores available on right
0.1	16.0	L	**Pound Ridge Rd. (Rt. 172)**
0.5	16.5	R	**Middle Patent Rd.** If you wish to avoid a steep dirt downhill, go **straight** on Rt. 172 for 0.2 miles and turn **right** toward Stamford on **Long Ridge Rd.** (no sign). In 0.6 miles, turn **right** on **Miller's Mill Rd.** Go 0.1 miles and turn left onto Mianus Rd., where you rejoin the main route at Mile 17.3
0.6	17.1	L	**Miller's Mill Rd.** CAUTION: Unpaved road with steep downhill
0.2	17.3	R	**Mianus Rd.**
0.6	17.9		**Mianus River gorge** hiking/nature area on left (no offroad bicycling allowed). Water and restrooms available
1.8	19.7	L	**E. Middle Patent Rd.** (T)
2.2	21.9	L	**Taconic Rd.** (T)
1.2	23.1	S	N. Stanwich Rd. goes right
0.8	23.9	BR	At "Y" onto **Stanwich Rd.**
0.3	24.2	R	**S. Stanwich Rd.** (cross lake)
0.6	24.8	R	**North St.** (T)
0.4	25.2	L	**Lower Cross Rd.**
1.5	26.7	BL	**Lake Ave.** (T)
0.1	26.8	R	**Burying Hill Rd.**
0.4	27.2	L	**Highland Farm Rd.**

Pt. to Point	Cume	Turn	Street/Landmark
0.5	27.7	L	**Cherry Valley Rd.** (T)
0.7	28.4	R	**Old Mill Rd.** (T)
0.7	29.1	S	Cross Round Hill Rd. at stop sign
0.8	29.9	R	**N. Porchuck Rd.** (T)
0.5	30.4	R	**Riversville Rd.** (stop sign)
0.4	30.8	L	**John St.**
0.7	31.5	L	**Bedford Rd.** (T)
1.1	32.6	R	**King St.** (T) **Fruit stand** on right after turn
0.5	33.1	L	**Gateway Lane (Rt. 120A)**
0.2	33.3	L	**Rt. 120 South**
0.6	33.9	L	**Westchester Airport** entrance road (at traffic light by I-684 entrance)
0.9	34.8	S	**Airport parking lot;** end of route

NORTH COUNTY TRAILWAY - 26.4 MILES

Terrain: Flat to very gentle along the bike path, then rolling to steep heading to the Hudson River and back through Sleepy Hollow country.

Traffic: Lots of bikes and walkers on the bike path (though most are going at a good clip!). Little traffic near Croton Reservoir. Light to moderate from Ossining back to Briarcliff Manor, except somewhat heavy on Route 9 and a short stretch of Route 117.

Road Conditions: Great on new paved bike path. Fair to good on the roads. One long and one short section of unpaved road, mostly hard-packed, on the main route can be skipped with paved alternates described in the cue sheet.

Points of Interest: North County Trailway, a bike path following the route of the old Putnam Railroad; **Kitchawan Research Station** of the Brooklyn Botanical Garden; Croton Reservoir area; old buildings of Ossining, including Sing Sing Prison; wealthy homes in Scarborough; Sleepy Hollow country cycling.

This new *RIDE GUIDE* route is adopted from White Plains-Croton Point, which appeared in the original edition of this book. It takes advantage of the North County Trailway, a bike path following the old Putnam Railroad. Currently, segments are missing between Eastview and Briarcliff Manor and Croton Reservoir to Yorktown. When the southerly missing link is completed, this route can be cycled all the way from Eastview, combining this route with Sleepy Hollow Special (page 41). New York State and Westchester are ambitiously attempting to create a rail-trail for the entire Putnam branch, from the Bronx to Putnam County.

Begin at the Briarcliff Manor Library, which used to be a handsome station along the "Old Put." The path follows the shoulder of Rt. 100 for a ways, but it is a very wide shoulder and traffic is light. At Millwood, pass another station then head "off-road" on the tree-shaded path, which at one point crosses over Rt. 100 on an overpass.

After riding to the path's dead end near the Croton Reservoir (ATB riders can brave the dirt to the shore of the reservoir), hit the road on Rt. 134 and then ride some pleasant, quiet downhill stretches alongside the reservoir. ATB and road bikers who don't mind a little dirt (mostly hard-packed) can continue for two miles along the reservoir with only an occasional fisherman's car as company.

NORTH COUNTY TRAILWAY
26.4 Miles

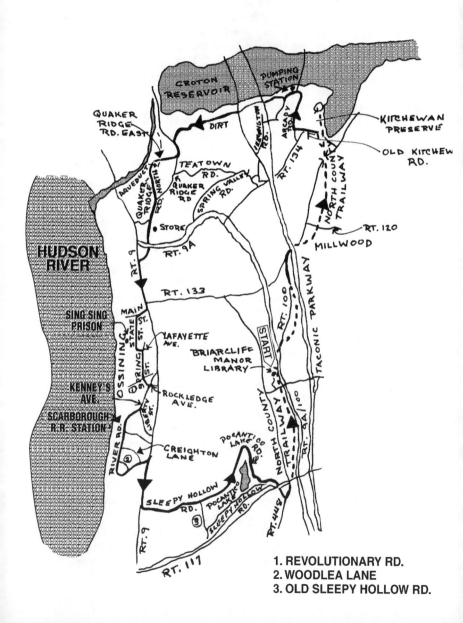

HUDSON RIVER

SING SING PRISON

KENNEY'S AVE.

SCARBOROUGH R.R. STATION

CROTON RESERVOIR

DUMPING STATION

QUAKER RIDGE RD. EAST

DIRT

KITCHEWAN PRESERVE

OLD KITCHEW RD.

TEATOWN RD.

QUAKER RIDGE RD

AQUEDUCT

QUAKER RIDGE RD. NORTH

SPRING VALLEY RD.

ILLINGTON RD.

ARCADY RD.

RT. 134

NORTH COUNTY TRAILWAY

RT. 120

MILLWOOD

Store

RT. 9A

RT. 9

RT. 133

OSSINING

MAIN STATE ST.

SPRING ST.

LAFAYETTE AVE.

BRIARCLIFF MANOR LIBRARY

START

RT. 100

TACONIC PARKWAY

ROCKLEDGE AVE.

LIBERTY ST.

RIVER RD.

CREIGHTON LANE

NORTH COUNTY TRAILWAY

RT. 9A/100

POCANTICO LAKE RD.

SLEEPY HOLLOW RD.

POCANTICO LAKE RD.

SLEEPY HOLLOW RD.

RT. 448

RT. 9

RT. 111

1. REVOLUTIONARY RD.
2. WOODLEA LANE
3. OLD SLEEPY HOLLOW RD.

Thin-tire folks who wish to skip this section are provided a paved alternate.

Cycle down near the Croton Gorge and on to Ossining. (Note of caution: it is advisable to ride in pairs through Ossining; if riding solo, use Rt. 9 instead. Take a peek at Sing Sing Prison, then head through wealthy Scarborough before going into Sleepy Hollow country. The Rockefellers are primarily responsible for the bucolic nature of the land near Pocantico.

The main route heads down a short but rough dirt road by Pocantico Lake. This is an extremely attractive stretch and is worth walking if you're not confident your wheels can take it, but another paved alternate is provided.

In less than a mile, you're back on the North County Trailway for the 1.7-mile zoom to the Briarcliff Manor Library.

Directions to Starting Point: The **Briarcliff Manor Library** is located on Pleasantville Road, just west of Rts. 9A/100. The easiest car approach is on the Taconic Pkwy. to the Pleasantville Road exit (motorists off northbound Rts. 9A/100 are not allowed to turn left at Pleasantville Rd.). Turn left, cross over Routes 9A/100, and turn right into the library driveway.

Metro-North Directions: Take a Hudson Line local to Scarborough. Turn right outside the station parking lot onto Kemeys Ave. The next turn will be at Mile 19.3 of the cue sheet. Ride to Briarcliff Manor then start the ride from the beginning.

Pt. to Point	Cume	Turn	Street/Landmark
0.0	0.0	L	Ride behind library and turn **left** onto **North County Trailway**
0.2	0.2		Cross Rt. 100. Ride on right shoulder
0.2	0.4		Watch for merging traffic coming from ramp
0.3	0.7	R	**Bike path**
1.6	2.3	R	Join shoulder of **Rt. 100**
0.6	2.9	S	At traffic light
0.1	3.0		Go under Taconic Parkway
0.2	3.2	R	Re-enter **North County Trailway**. Easy to miss
0.6	3.8	S	Pass old Millwood train station on left. Carefully cross Rt. 120
2.0	5.8	BR	At fork, going under Rt. 134

Pt. to Point	Cume	Turn	Street/Landmark
0.2	6.0		**U-turn** at end of paved path. Nice view of reservoir
0.2	6.2	SR	After underpass, heading up toward Rt. 134
0.1	6.3	L	**Rt. 134 West**
0.5	6.8		**Brooklyn Botanic Garden Kitchawan Preserve** on right
0.2	7.0	R	**Old Kitchawan Rd.**
0.4	7.4	SR	**Arcady Rd.** Turn comes up fast as you are coming down hill. Continue down hill
1.3	8.7	S	At huge New York City water pumping station. Continue along reservoir
0.5	9.2	R	At unmarked intersection, onto **dirt road following reservoir**. For paved alternate, turn **left** here and climb 0.3 miles. Turn **right**, cross Taconic Parkway, then turn **left** on **Illington Rd.** In about a mile, you will arrive at **Rt. 134**. Turn **right** on **Grants Lane** (just before Rt. 134), then in 0.1 miles make another **right** on unmarked **Spring Valley Rd.** at T (toward Teatown Reservation). In 0.7 miles, take a right onto **Teatown Rd.** (just past lake on right), and climb a steep hill. In 1.8 miles, make a left onto **Quaker Ridge Rd.**, and in 1 mile turn left onto **Quaker Bridge Rd.** and rejoin main route. The next turn will be at Mile 15.2
2.0	11.2		Pavement returns. Start to climb
0.6	11.8	BL	At yield sign onto **Quaker Ridge Rd.** (no street sign)
1.0	12.8	R	**Quaker Bridge Rd. East**. Down steep, curvy road
0.4	13.2		Cross Croton Aqueduct path
0.2	13.4	L	Where narrow bridge goes off to the right, onto unmarked **Quaker Bridge Rd. North.** Climb
0.4	13.8		Aqueduct path crosses
0.7	14.5	S	At intersection, onto **Quaker Bridge Rd.** Road changes name to **Old Albany Post Rd.**

Pt. to Point	Cume	Turn	Street/Landmark
0.7	15.2	S	At stop sign where Samstag Ave. comes off to the left. Deli on left
0.2	15.4		Go under Route 9A
0.2	15.6	L	**N. Highland Ave. (Rt. 9 South)** (traffic light)
1.5	17.1	R	**Main St., Ossining.** *If riding solo, it is best to skip Ossining section. Continue on Rt. 9 South for about a mile, and bear right onto Revolutionary Rd. Rejoin main route at Mile 18.8*
0.0	17.1	BR	At fork, to continue on **Main St.**
0.2	17.3	L	**State St.** (no sign). Turn is before a steep descent
0.5	17.8		**Sing Sing Prison** on right
0.1	17.9	L	**Lafayette Ave.**
0.1	18.0	R	**Spring St.**
0.4	18.4	S	At stop sign. Cross Liberty St. onto **Rockledge Ave.**
0.2	18.6	R	**Revolutionary Rd.**
0.2	18.8	R	**Kemeys Ave.** (stop sign)
0.4	19.2		**Scarborough Railroad Station** on right
0.1	19.3	BR	**River Rd.**
0.7	20.0	BR	To continue on **River Rd.** (Woodlea Lane goes left)
0.1	20.1	BR	To continue on **River Rd.** (Creighton Lane goes left)
0.2	20.3	R	**Rt. 9** (T)
0.5	20.8	L	**Sleepy Hollow Rd.**
1.2	22.0	L	At fork where Old Sleepy Hollow Rd. goes right (if you wish to avoid dirt, turn **right** here instead; go 0.5 miles to intersection of Sleepy Hollow Rd. and turn left. You are one mile before the intersection at Mile 23.4)
0.7	22.7	SR	At second intersection of **Old Sleepy Hollow Rd.** Ignore "No Outlet" sign. Slow down, road becomes a poor, bumpy dirt road at bottom of hill. Walk if necessary — it's worth it, a beautiful lakeside road adjacent to Pocantico Lake
0.5	23.2	L	At fork, onto unmarked **Pocantico Lake Rd.** Pavement returns
0.2	23.4	L	**Sleepy Hollow Rd.** (T)

Pt. to Point	Cume	Turn	Street/Landmark
0.5	23.9	S	Under Rt.117 expressway underpass
0.4	24.3	L	**Rt. 448** (T) (yield sign)
0.1	24.4	R	**Rt. 117** (traffic light). Watch for heavy traffic
0.3	24.7	L	Onto **bike path**. Turn is opposite Mount Pleasant Pool and just before intersection of Routes 9A/100. During road construction, use extreme caution. Path entrance may be easy to miss. Walk left turn
1.7	26.4	L	Off bike path after Pleasantville Rd. underpass into **Briarcliff Manor Public Library**. End of route

RIDES STARTING IN NORTHERN WESTCHESTER

Pedalers who ride frequently in Westchester usually head north because it is still big and open and sparsely developed, though a lot less so than when the first edition of *RIDE GUIDE/ Hudson Valley and Sound Shore* was published in 1986. Thanks to the thirsty souls of New York City, there are still lots of woods surrounding the Croton Watershed reservoirs, although there has been some talk of selling development rights. This is a hilly section: bring your best pair of quadriceps to the starting points.

Armonk-Purdys roughly follows the route of Interstate 684, but you will be using remote back roads out of earshot of the big highway. Along the way are several fine nature preserves, country stores, an elephant atop a pedestal, and Reader's Digest headquarters. The main attraction of this and other routes in Northern Westchester are miles of traffic-free back roads in the woods and alongside reservoirs.

New England plays a major role in shaping the scenery along the **Bedford-Ridgefield** route. Bedford used to be in Connecticut, and Ridgefield still is. The stone walls and rocky terrain commonly found from Massachusetts to Maine are in abundance in Pound Ridge, N.Y. and vicinity. Look for large, modern homes of unique design hiding deep in wooded lots.

Like to eat fruit and drink wine? Then you'll enjoy **Katonah-North Salem**, which passes an orchard and a vineyard. This pedal also features Ward Pound Ridge Reservation, the county's largest park (trails closed to ATBs, but a fine paved road through it), and Caramoor, a mansion known for its concerts and formal gardens.

Two rides leave from the convenient Croton-Harmon rail station, and directions are given to combine them into one longer route. **Croton-Mohansic** heads to Mohansic Lake in Franklin D. Roosevelt State Park by way of Croton Dam and a pick-your-own orchard on top of a challenging hill. For more mileage, cycle north from Yorktown Heights car-free on a 5.5-mile stretch of the North County Trailway. On the way back, be sure to visit Teatown Reservation, an excellent nature preserve with a lake and museum. **Croton To The Point** visits the little-known village of

Verplanck. Excellent river views can be seen here and for those interested, there's an energy exhibit at the nearby Indian Point nuclear power plant. Enroute to "the Point," stop at Blue Mountain Reservation for a swim at the small lake beach.

Either Croton ride is convenient for a visit to Van Cortlandt Manor, the home of 18th Century Westchester aristocracy. Directions are given in the Croton To The Point ride for a visit to Croton Point Park, the coolest spot in the county on hot summer days, thanks to breezes off the Hudson.

If you wish to tour extreme northwestern Westchester (and well up into Putnam County), head for the **Peekskill Hollow Ride**. This route follows narrow river valleys through remote sections of Putnam, aiming for Clarence Fahnstock Park with its excellent beach and picnic areas. On the way back you pass Westchester's only water slide at Sprout Brook Park.

For ATBers, Northern Westchester offers two excellent choices — **Blue Mountain Reservation**, a county park in Peekskill, contains several miles of trails open to fat-tire cyclists, but be ready for challenge as these trails are rocky and hilly. **Croton Aqueduct** is more for novices — it is a delight, running high above the pipes that supply New York City with water, following the flat right-of-way used for aqueduct maintenance, with excellent views of the Hudson just to the west.

ARMONK-PURDYS - 49.0 MILES

Terrain: Considering this is Northern Westchester, not too bad. Mostly rolling, a few steep climbs. The return trip, however, contains some memorable ascents on Crow Hill Rd., Rt. 133 and Whippoorwill Rd.

Traffic: Very light, except moderate between Purdys and Somers and on Rt. 133

Road Conditions: Very good, except dirt on Old Roaring Brook Rd.

Points of Interest: Butler and Westmoreland Sanctuaries (hiking; nature study; no ATBs); Caramoor (museum, garden, concerts); general store in **Purdys** (an old-fashioned general store friendly to cyclists); the **Somers Elephant; Reader's Digest headquarters** (tour with artworks open to public on weekdays); **Whippoorwill Rd. area** (beautiful homes and views).

It is possible to drive from Armonk to Purdys in under 20 minutes on Interstate 684. A much better way to travel between these two towns is on two wheels, exploring the many quiet roads in this affluent, still lightly settled area.

Start in Armonk, a pleasant town of shops that is home to IBM's world headquarters. Head north on roads that parallel I-684, but are generally not within earshot of the highway. Two excellent nature preserves, Butler and Westmoreland Sanctuaries, are located six miles into the route.

The next point of interest is Caramoor. This mansion is known for its formal gardens, concerts and house tour. Continue north on numbered highways which are remarkably free of traffic. Ride along pretty Titicus Reservoir into tiny Purdys. The store here has a front porch ideal for eating lunch, and is a frequent destination of local cyclists.

The return route takes you by a large pedestal in Somers, atop which is a statue of an elephant. This town is considered a birthplace of the circus in this country. Hachaliah Bailey, whose descendents later joined with Barnum, owned the hotel on the corner here, named in honor of his elephant Bet, which was the first elephant in the U.S.

ARMONK-PURDYS
49.0 Miles

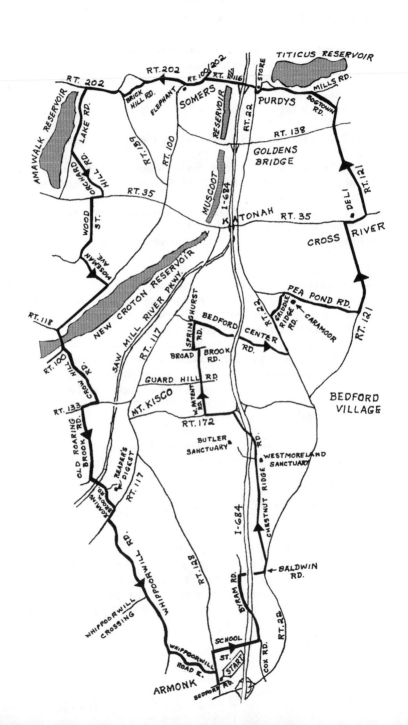

Enjoy quiet backroads in the region of New York City's Croton watershed as you ride by Amawalk and Croton reservoirs. A few climbs and descents later (one of which, on Old Roaring Brook Rd., requires caution due to lack of pavement!), cycle by Reader's Digest headquarters. This imposing colonial structure contains exhibits open to the public on weekdays.

The final stretch of this route is over Whippoorwill Rd. This is definitely hilly, but the views, open fields, woods, and opulent homes make the exertion worthwhile.

Directions to Starting Point: The ride begins at the intersection of **Rt. 128 and Bedford Rd.** in the center of Armonk. Take I-684 to Exit 3, then Rt. 22 South to the second traffic light and turn right. Parking is available on the streets of Armonk or in municipal lots.

Metro-North Directions: (approx. 6 miles each way from station to start of ride): Take a Harlem Division local or express to North White Plains. Exit onto Fisher Lane and turn right. Ride to Rt. 22 and turn left. Follow Rt. 22 to Rt. 128 and turn left. The ride begins in several blocks at the intersection of Bedford Rd.

Note: It is possible to combine this route with the Greenwich-Armonk ride (page 33) to make a challenging 82.1-mile circuit. See the note following the description of the Greenwich-Armonk route for the best directions.

Pt. to Point	Cume	Turn	Street/Landmark
0.0	0.0	L	From the intersection of Rt. 128 and Bedford Rd., ride **north** on **Rt. 128**
0.6	0.6	R	**School St.**
0.9	1.5	SL	**Byram Rd.** (no sign; Sunset Rd. goes off to the right beyond the turn) (riders from Greenwich join here)
2.5	4.0	R	**Baldwin Rd.** (no sign; turn at a road which immediately goes under I-684 and climbs a hill)
0.4	4.4	L	**Rt. 22** (T)
0.1	4.5	L	**Chestnut Ridge Rd.**
1.5	6.0	S	Road to **Butler Sanctuary** goes left. **Westmoreland Sanctuary** is on the right
1.3	7.3	L	**Rt. 172** (T)
0.9	8.2	R	**W. Patent Rd.**

Pt. to Point	Cume	Turn	Street/Landmark
0.8	9.0	S	Cross Guard Hill Rd.
0.8	9.8	L	**Broad Brook Rd.** (T)
0.1	9.9	R	**Springhurst Rd.**
0.6	10.5	R	**Bedford Center Rd.** (T)
2.6	13.1	L	At fork onto **Rt. 22** (no sign) (Bedford Cross sign is on the island of the fork)
1.5	14.6	R	**Girdle Ridge Rd.**
0.5	15.1	R	**Pea Pond Rd.** (T) (no sign)
0.2	15.3		**Caramoor Center for Music and the Arts** on the right
2.0	17.3	L	**Old Post Rd. (Rt. 121)** (T)
2.4	19.7	R	To continue on **Rt. 121/35 East** (T). Deli on left after turn
0.6	20.3	L	To continue on **Rt. 121 North** (traffic light; Rt. 35 goes straight)
2.6	22.9	S	Cross Rt. 138
0.7	23.6	BL	**Bogtown Rd.** Road changes name to **Mills Rd.**
2.5	26.1	BL	At unmarked fork to continue on **Mills Rd.**
0.4	26.5	L	**Main St.** (T) (no sign; **Purdys; general store** on right after turn)
0.1	26.6	R	**Rt. 22** (T)
0.0	26.6	L	Immediate **left** onto **Rt. 116 West**
1.5	28.1	BL	**Rt. 202 West** (stop sign)
0.3	28.4	R	At fork to continue on **Rt. 202** (note **elephant statue** on side of road)
1.4	29.8	L	**Brick Hill Rd.**
0.5	30.3	R	**Rt. 139** (at fork and stop sign)
0.1	30.4	L	**Rt. 202 West**
0.6	31.0	L	**Lake Rd.** (first left after Lincoln Hall School)
1.8	32.8	L	**Orchard Hill Rd.** (road goes up hill immediately)
1.5	34.3	R	**Rt. 35** (T)
0.3	34.6	L	**Wood St.**
1.5	36.1	L	**Moseman Ave.** (T)
0.7	36.8	R	**Rt. 100** (T)
1.9	38.7	S	At traffic light to continue on **Rt. 100 South**. Cross bridge over reservoir
0.4	39.1	L	**Crow Hill Rd.** (traffic light)
1.9	41.0	R	**Rt. 133** (T)
0.5	41.5	L	**Old Roaring Brook Rd.**

Pt. to Point	Cume	Turn	Street/Landmark
0.6	42.1		Road turns to dirt for 0.5 miles, then pavement returns. Use caution on downhill stretches
1.3	43.4	L	Turn toward the traffic light and cross Saw Mill River Pkwy. heading toward the Reader's Digest building
0.2	43.6	R	**Roaring Brook Rd.** (turn is in front of the Reader's Digest building)
0.4	44.0	R	**Rt. 117** (T) (traffic light; no street sign)
0.4	44.4	L	**Whippoorwill Rd.**
2.1	46.5	S	At Whippoorwill Crossing. Enjoy a nice view!
1.5	48.0	L	**Whippoorwill Rd. East**
0.9	48.9	R	**Rt. 128** (traffic light)
0.1	49.0		Intersection of **Rt. 128 and Bedford Rd.** (end of route)

BEDFORD-RIDGEFIELD - 27.5 MILES

Terrain: Rolling. A few hills, but nothing that most cyclists will have trouble with.
Traffic: Light, except moderate near Ridgefield.
Road Conditions: Excellent, with some bumpy pavement near Ridgefield and about 0.8 miles of dirt road
Points of Interest: Historic **Bedford Village**; New Englandy **Ridgefield** (large homes, Aldrich Museum and nice shops); a very quiet corner of Westchester to ride in.

The towns of Pound Ridge and Lewisboro occupy much of the land in the zigzag border between New York and Connecticut — land that was once part of New England but now is Westchester territory.

The New England influence is seen in the stone walls that abound in the woods. These walls once separated farm fields, before forests and opulent homes took over. Cyclists will be especially impressed with the amount of rock visible on the appropriately named Old Stone Hill Rd.

Ridgefield is a "real" New England town with large, stately homes and a collection of shops catering to a well-to-do clientele. There is only one sit-down eatery in town (a coffee shop located off of Main Street to the right beyond town hall, on Bailey Ave.), but there are several delicatessens and a cart called Le Hot Dog for al fresco dining.

Return via the miniature hamlet of Vista on the New York-Connecticut state line, then through Pound Ridge, which has street signs that look like pointing arms. Be sure to walk around Bedford Village, which has numerous historic homes and an 18th-century courthouse and museum.

Directions to Starting Point: Bedford Village is in northeastern Westchester County. Take Exit 4 off I-684, then follow Rt. 172 East to Rt. 22 North. Turn right on Court Rd., just beyond the Bedford Village green, and park beyond the 2-hour parking signs.
Metro-North Directions: (about 7 miles each way from the station): Take a Harlem Division train bound for Brewster North

BEDFORD-RIDGEFIELD
27.5 Miles

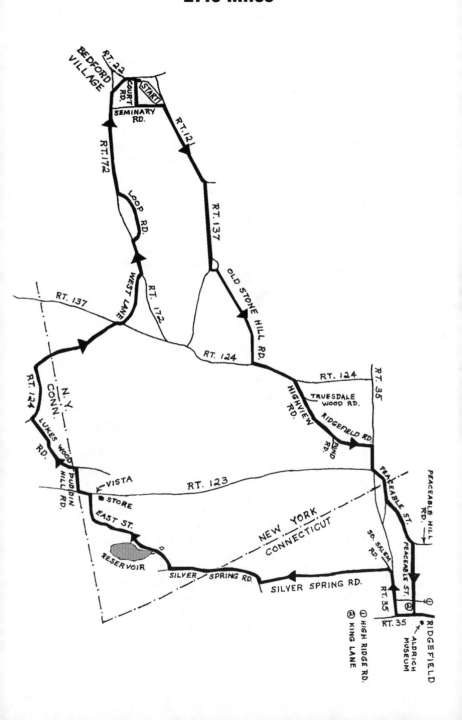

to the Mt. Kisco station. Cycle east to Main St., then south on Rt.
117 to Rt. 172. Ride east on Rt. 172 to Rt. 22, then north to
Bedford Village. Note that traffic can be heavy on Rt. 172.
*Note: You can combine this route with the Westchester Airport-
Bedford ride (page 52) for a 62.3-mile route, a perfect metric
century.*

Pt. to Point	Cume	Turn	Street/Landmark
0.0	0.0	L	Start at the intersection of **Court Rd. and Rt. 22**. Ride on **Court Rd.**, away from Rt. 22
0.3	0.3	L	**Seminary Rd.** (T)
0.2	0.5	R	**Rt. 121** (T)
1.4	1.9	R	**Rt. 137 South**
2.0	3.9	L	**Old Stone Hill Rd.**
0.0	3.9	BR	At fork immediately after last turn to continue on **Old Stone Hill Rd.**
1.7	5.6	L	**Rt. 124** (T)
1.0	6.6	R	**Highview Rd.**
0.3	6.9	BR	At fork. Truesdale Wood Rd. goes left
1.0	7.9	S	At stop sign (Pond Rd. goes right). Name of the road you are on changes to **Ridgefield Rd.**
0.6	8.5	R	**Rt. 35** (stop sign)
0.3	8.8	L	**Peaceable St.** (Rt. 123 goes right at this intersection)
0.3	9.1	L	Turn beyond Pinchbeck Bros. Florist to continue on **Peaceable St.** (street sign says "Old S. Salem Rd.")
0.6	9.7	R	At first intersection to stay on **Peaceable St**. Peaceable Hill Rd. goes straight
1.0	10.7	BR	Cross High Ridge Rd. You are now on **King Lane**
0.2	10.9	L	**Rt. 35 North** (T). **Aldrich Museum of Contemporary Art** on right after turn
0.5	11.4		Turn around at the end of downtown **Ridgefield** and cycle back on **Rt. 35 South**
0.8	12.2	R	To continue on **Rt. 35 South**
0.8	13.0	L	**South Salem Rd.** (green sign at the intersection points right for New York)
0.0	13.0	L	**Silver Spring Rd.**
1.4	14.4	R	Continue on **Silver Spring Rd.** (T; no sign)

Pt. to Point	Cume	Turn	Street/Landmark
2.0	16.4		Road turns to dirt upon entering New York State
0.2	16.6	R	**East St.** (first right turn after road becomes dirt)
0.6	17.2		Pavement returns
1.6	18.8	L	**Rt. 123** (T). If you wish to go to a store, turn right here instead and ride about one block into downtown Vista. Store is on the right
0.1	18.9	R	**Puddin Hill Rd.**
0.3	19.2	L	**Lukes Wood Rd.** (T; no sign). West Rd. goes right
1.0	20.2	R	**Rt. 124** (T)
2.9	23.1	BR	**Rt. 137**
0.0	23.1	L	Immediate **left** onto **West Lane**
0.8	23.9	L	**Rt. 172** (T; no sign)
1.1	25.0	R	**Loop Rd.**
0.5	25.5	R	**Rt. 172** (T; no sign)
1.9	27.4	R	At Bedford Green onto **Rt. 22**
0.1	27.5		Intersection of **Court Rd. and Rt. 22**. End of route

KATONAH-NORTH SALEM - 34.4 MILES

Terrain: Rolling, at times quite steeply. Expect some long ascents and descents.
Traffic: Light, except for Rt. 35 near the beginning and end of the ride
Road Conditions: Excellent, when paved. Expect about a mile of dirt roads, including a steep dirt climb on Post Rd.
Points of Interest: Quiet roads and **fantastic vistas** of North and South Salem; **Waccabuc** post office, the smallest in the U.S.; a **vineyard** and **pick-your-own orchard** on Hardscrabble Rd.; **Ward Pound Ridge Reservation** (hiking, picnics and trailside museum; no ATB riding); **Caramoor** (gardens, museum and concerts); **John Jay Homestead.**

The northeast corner of Westchester, while growing due to the presence of I-684, is still lightly settled and contains delightful riding. There are hills here, but who can forget the sight of Lake Waccabuc nestled in the valley? Your legs will forgive you.

Ride out of busy Katonah and head north for Goldens Bridge and Somers. Look for the elephant on the pedestal in Somers; this was where the first circus in the U.S. was organized. The statue was put up by Hachaliah Bailey. Next head up toward Croton Falls. For lovers of fruit and fruits of the vine, Hardscrabble Rd. has Outhouse Orchards (so named because the owner is Mr. Outhouse) and the North Salem Vineyard.

After passing through North Salem, head toward South Salem by way of Waccabuc. That tiny building on Post Office Rd. is one of the smallest post offices in the country. Buy some food at the store in South Salem, and ride several miles further to Ward Pound Ridge Reservation for a picnic. This is Westchester's largest and most beautiful park, with many miles of wooded hilltop and streamside hiking trails and an excellent trailside museum. Although these trails seem tempting, they are off-limits to fat-tire bicycles.

Return to Katonah by way of Caramoor (a museum noted for its concerts and beautiful garden) and the home of John Jay, our first Supreme Court Chief Justice.

KATONAH-NORTH SALEM
33.4 Miles

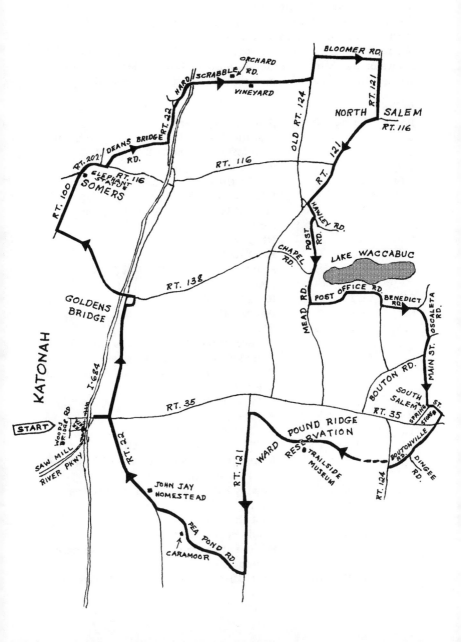

Directions to Starting Point: Katonah is located at the junction of I-684 and NY 35. Drivers coming from the Tappan Zee Bridge may use the Saw Mill River Pkwy. to reach I-684. Take Exit 6 and turn left on Rt. 35. Turn left onto Woods Bridge Rd. and then make the first right into the Woods Bridge parking area, where the route begins. If the lot is full, parking is legal on the shoulder of Rt. 35 on the railroad overpass.

Metro-North Directions: Take a Harlem Division train bound for Brewster North to the Katonah station. Proceed left one block to Woods Bridge Rd., then turn right to the start of the route.

Pt. to Point	Cume	Turn	Street/Landmark
0.0	0.0	L	Exit the Woods Bridge parking area and turn **left** onto **Woods Bridge Rd.**
0.2	0.2	R	**Rt. 35** (traffic light)
0.6	0.8	L	**Rt. 22 North** (first traffic light past I-684 intersections)
2.1	2.9	R	Toward **Rt. 138** (by A&P shopping center)
0.2	3.1	L	**Rt. 138** (T)
1.9	5.0	R	**Rt. 100 North** (T)
0.9	5.9	S	At traffic light onto **Rt. 202 East** (note **elephant** statue on right)
0.3	6.2	R	**Rt. 116 East**
0.1	6.3	L	**Deans Bridge Rd.** (Rt. 116 curves right)
1.3	7.6	L	**Rt. 22** (T)
0.5	8.1	R	**Hardscrabble Rd.** (fork; no sign; follow signs for I-684. Rt. 22 goes left). **Outhouse Orchards** will be on the left in one mile
3.5	11.6	L	At "Y" onto **Old Rt. 124**
0.4	12.0	R	**Bloomer Rd.**
1.3	13.3	R	**Rt. 121** (T)
1.2	14.5	BR	At T, to continue on **Rt. 121**
1.1	15.6	BL	At fork, to continue on **Rt. 121 South** (Rt. 116 goes right)
0.9	16.5	L	**Hawley Rd.** (toward Mountain Lakes Camp)
0.1	16.6	R	**Post Rd.**
0.2	16.8		Road becomes dirt
0.4	17.2		Pavement returns. Road changes name to **Mead St.**
1.6	18.8	L	**Post Office Rd.** One of the smallest post

Pt. to Point	Cume	Turn	Street/Landmark
			offices in the U.S. is on the right after the turn
1.0	19.8	L	**Benedict Rd.**
0.8	20.6	R	At "Y" and yield sign onto **Oscaleta Rd.** (no street sign)
0.6	21.2	R	**Main St.** (T)
1.1	22.3	BL	**Spring St.** (stop sign)
0.1	22.4		Store on right
0.2	22.6	R	**Boutonville Rd.**
0.1	22.7	S	Cross Rt. 35
0.5	23.2		Road becomes dirt
0.5	23.7	BR	At fork to continue on **Boutonville Rd.** (Dingee Rd. goes left)
0.1	23.8		Pavement returns
0.2	24.0	R	**Rt. 124** (T)
0.1	24.1	L	At first paved road into **Ward Pound Ridge Reservation** (not a car entrance). Walk bike around pillars with chain across and ride into park
1.3	25.4		**Trailside Museum** on left
1.4	26.8	L	**Rt. 121** (T)
2.4	29.2	R	**Pea Pond Rd.**
2.0	31.2		**Caramoor Center for Music and the Arts** on the left
0.6	31.8	BR	At yield sign onto **Rt. 22 North**
0.2	32.0		**John Jay Homestead** on right
1.6	33.6	L	**Rt. 35 West** (traffic light)
0.6	34.2	L	**Woods Bridge Rd.** (first traffic light past I-684 intersections)
0.2	34.4	R	**Woods Bridge parking area** (end of route)

CROTON-MOHANSIC - 33.0 MILES, PLUS 11 MILE SPUR

Terrain: Rolling, with a few extremely steep hills. The North County Trailway spur is basically one continuous moderate upgrade heading north, a big zoom south.
Traffic: Moderate near Croton, moderate to heavy on Rt. 202 into Yorktown, otherwise light. Only bikes, in-line skaters and walkers on the bike path.
Road Conditions: Very good.
Points of Interest: Croton Gorge Park underneath the huge Croton Dam; **Wilkens Farm** pick-your-own apples (fall); **F.D. Roosevelt (Mohansic) Park** (swimming and boating); **North County Trailway (north section); Teatown Lake Reservation** (hiking and nature museum); **Van Cortlandt Manor** (a Sleepy Hollow restoration).

Two of the more challenging climbs in Westchester are included in this route, yet novice cyclists should not reject this ride because overall the terrain is merely "rolling." The western end of the Croton Reservoir watershed contains some beautiful wooded and quiet back roads, and the two hard ascents can easily be walked since there is little traffic at those points.

Start by cycling out of Croton up quiet, residential streets. Take a short detour into Croton Gorge park to see the Croton Dam, an impressive concrete structure worth a photograph if a lot of water is flowing over the spillway. Off-road cyclists coming by train to the Croton Aqueduct ride (see page 93) leave the route here to hit the dirt.

Cross the reservoir on a bridge, then head north along an arm on the lake on quiet Hunter Brook Rd. Turn right to climb Big Hill No. 1. The sound of a stream down in the ravine is soothing during the struggle against gravity. Reward yourself at the top with fresh fruit at Wilkens Farm if you are riding in the late summer or fall.

Next head over to F.D. Roosevelt Park, where you can picnic on a meadow overlooking Mohansic Lake, rent a boat, or swim in the pool. Ride through busy Yorktown Heights, where you can leave the suburban pace of this growing area for a 11-mile round trip

CROTON-MOHANSIC
34.0 Miles, Plus 11 Mile Spur

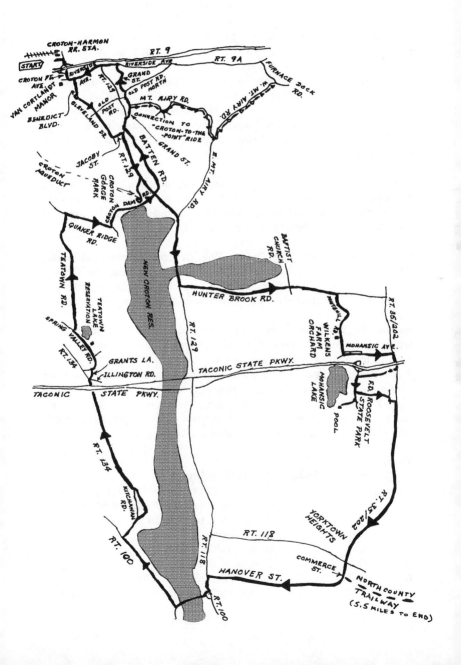

on the bucolic north section of the North County Trailway, a smoothly-paved expanse of former railroad right-of-way.

Back on the main route, head up Hanover St., past one of the county's few working dairy farms. Return to Croton Reservoir, crossing it on the Rt. 100 bridge. The next stop is Teatown Lake Reservation, a beautiful nature preserve with an interesting museum. The roads in this section are virtually traffic-free, which is a good thing because you must climb Big Hill No. 2 right after Teatown. This ascent is much shorter than No. 1, but quite a bit steeper. On top you will enjoy a ride down a European-looking one-lane road past lovely backwoodsy homes and horse farms. You will emerge on top of Croton Dam and only 4 1/2 miles from the end of the route.

Van Cortlandt Manor, a Sleepy Hollow restoration, is located near the Croton-Harmon station. You may buy a combined ticket that will admit you to Sunnyside and Philipsburg Manor, located on the Sleepy Hollow Special route (page 41).

Directions to Starting Point: The **Croton-Harmon Railroad Station** is located off Rt. 9, north of Ossining. Take the Croton Point Ave. exit. Turn left if coming off northbound Rt. 9 and right if coming off southbound Rt. 9. The station parking lot is on the left.

Metro-North Directions: Take a Hudson Line local or express train to Croton-Harmon. The ride begins at the top of the road exiting from the station parking lot.

Note: The cue sheet includes a link to the Croton To The Point route (page 84). Following this link, you can have a 54.4- or 56.8-mile ride. The link (Mt. Airy Rd.) goes up-up-up, then down-down-down, but the bad hills fade away eventually as you get into the Croton To The Point ride and settle into a more moderate roll.

Pt. to Point	Cume	Turn	Street/Landmark
0.0	0.0	R	From the top of the hill at the exit from the Croton-Harmon Railroad Station parking lot, turn **right** onto **Croton Point Ave.**
0.2	0.2	L	**S. Riverside Ave.** (T; no sign)
0.1	0.3	R	**Benedict Blvd.**
0.2	0.5	L	At traffic circle, onto **Cleveland Dr.**
0.7	1.2	S	At stop sign, to continue on **Cleveland Dr.**

Pt.to Point	Cume	Turn	Street/Landmark
			Cross Old Post Rd.; Radnor Rd. goes left. You will have a cemetery on your left after passing this intersection
0.6	1.8	L	**Jacoby St.**
0.1	1.9	R	**Rt. 129** (T)
1.0	2.9	R	Into **Croton Gorge Park**
0.3	3.2		**U-turn** in parking lot at the foot of the dam and ride back up the way you came. *Riders heading to Croton Aqueduct, keep going to the last parking lot and start the Croton Aqueduct route there (page 95).*
0.3	3.5	R	**Rt. 129** (T)
1.9	5.4	L	**Hunter Brook Rd.** (just past bridge over reservoir)
2.0	7.4	S	Cross Baptist Church Rd.
1.5	8.9	R	**Whitehall Rd.** (turn is at bottom of hill after crossing a stone bridge). You will soon begin climbing a long, very steep hill
0.7	9.6		**Wilkens Farm** (pick your own apples) on right
0.2	9.8	L	**Mohansic Ave.** (stop sign; second left turn at intersection)
0.9	10.7	R	**Rts. 35/202** (T)
0.3	11.0	R	Before bus shelter (after crossing under Taconic Pkwy.), walk bike around wooden barricade to enter **F.D. Roosevelt State Park**. Pedal down park road paralleling Taconic Pkwy.
0.7	11.7	BL	At fork, toward **pool**. You will pass the nicest lunch spot (a meadow overlooking Mohansic Lake, near the boathouse) on this leg
0.5	12.2	BR	At fork, toward **pool**
0.2	12.4		**Pool** bathhouse. **U-turn** and ride back the way you came
0.1	12.5	BL	At fork, toward **picnic area**
0.4	12.9	R	Toward **Commercial Vehicle Exit**
0.7	13.6	BR	At fork, toward **Commercial Vehicle Exit**
0.1	13.7	L	Toward **Commercial Vehicle Exit**
0.2	13.9	R	**Rts. 35/202** toward Yorktown Heights

Pt. to Point	Cume	Turn	Street/Landmark
2.3	16.2	S	At traffic light, onto **Commerce St.** (no street sign)
0.4	16.6	S	Road changes name to **Hanover St.** as you leave the center of Yorktown Heights
0.3	16.9		Turn **left** just past the firehouse if you wish to ride the **North County Trailway**. Ride 5.5 miles straight to the end, then U-turn and ride 5.5 miles back. Use caution at road crossings
2.8	19.7	L	**Rt. 118** (T)
0.2	19.9	R	**Rt. 100 South** (T; traffic light). Cross reservoir
1.8	21.7	R	**Rt. 134**
0.9	22.6	R	**Kitchawan Rd.**
0.5	23.1	R	**Rt. 134** (T)
0.9	24.0	BR	**Grants Lane** (first turn after Taconic Pkwy. underpass; Illington Rd. is the sharp right)
0.1	24.1	R	**Spring Valley Rd.** (T) (no street sign; sign for Teatown Reservation)
0.6	24.7	BL	To continue on **Spring Valley Rd.** (Blinn Rd. goes left)
0.1	24.8		**Teatown Reservation** on right
0.6	25.4	R	**Teatown Rd.** (no sign; first right turn after passing lake on right. Climb ridiculously steep hill immediately)
1.8	27.2	R	**Quaker Ridge Rd.** (T; no sign)
1.3	28.5	L	**Croton Dam Rd.** (no sign; turn is at a fork with a big red house directly in front of you. You will cross over Croton Dam
0.9	29.4	S	Cross Rt. 129 onto **Batten Rd.**
1.4	30.8	R	**Rt. 129** (T)
0.3	31.1	R	**Grand St.**
0.2	31.3		*Turn **right** onto **Mt. Airy Rd.** if you are riding the joint 54.4- or 56.8-mile route out of Croton. See directions below.* Go **straight** here to continue the 33-mile Croton-Mohansic route
0.2	31.5	BL	At St. Augustine's Church to continue on **Grand St.** (no sign; Old Post Rd. North goes right; turn is first left past traffic light in Croton

Pt. to Point	Cume	Turn	Street/Landmark
0.5	32.0	L	**Riverside Ave.** (T)
0.8	32.8	R	**Croton Point Ave.** (toward railroad station). Go **straight** at this intersection if you wish to visit **Van Cortlandt Manor**
0.2	33.0	L	Into **Croton-Harmon Railroad Station** parking lot. End of route

DIRECTIONS FOR LINK TO CROTON TO THE POINT RIDE:

	Cume	Turn	Street/Landmark
	31.3	*R*	*Mt. Airy Rd.*
0.5	*31.8*	*L*	*Curve **left** to continue on **Mt. Airy Rd.** (Riverview, Mountain and Park Trails go right)*
0.8	*32.6*	*L*	*W. Mt. Airy Rd. (T)*
1.4	*34.0*	*R*	*Furnace Dock Rd. (yield sign)*

You are now on the Croton to the Point route. Continue on that route's cue sheet.

CROTON TO THE POINT - 24.7 OR 27.1 MILES

Terrain: Moderately rolling. One extended climb (Furnace Dock Rd.)

Traffic: Moderate, with light traffic up Furnace Dock Rd. and Maple Ave., out on "The Point" and near Crugers.

Road Conditions: Good, but the roads are occasionally treated with oil and stones, which makes for somewhat messy cycling.

Points of Interest: Blue Mountain Reservation (swimming, hiking, off-road riding (see route on page 97); **Indian Point energy exhibit**; good views of the Hudson at **Verplanck** and **Georges Island Park; Van Cortlandt Manor** (a Sleepy Hollow restoration); **Croton Point Park**.

Maps of the Hudson Valley drawn in the 18th Century call the large peninsula jutting out into the river north of Croton Verplanck's Point. Newer maps and the Consolidated Edison people call it Indian Point. Many locals refer to it simply as "the Point." Whatever you call it, this area of little-known villages and nice river views makes for good cycling.

Start by heading north out of Croton on Riverside Ave. Several nice river views are available before you turn inland (and uphill) on Furnace Dock Rd. Cycle through pleasant wooded countryside before heading back down toward the river and through a residential corner of Peekskill.

Blue Mountain Reservation is well worth a stop for its clean lake beach (generally open weekends only), picnic areas and hiking and off-road biking trails. Next, head toward the Indian Point nuclear generating plant. Con Edison runs an energy exhibit here that is open 10:00 a.m. to 5:00 p.m. Tues.-Sat. Enter at the main gate.

Past the nuclear plant is the quiet village of Verplanck. Enjoy the river views here and at Georges Island Park in nearby Montrose. The park has excellent picnic facilities.

Cycle into quiet Crugers and through a huge chunk of undeveloped parkland (Oscawana Park) with more excellent river views before returning to Croton-Harmon. You might wish to stop at the restored Van Cortlandt Manor near the end of the tour. At the

CROTON TO THE POINT
24.7 or 27 Miles

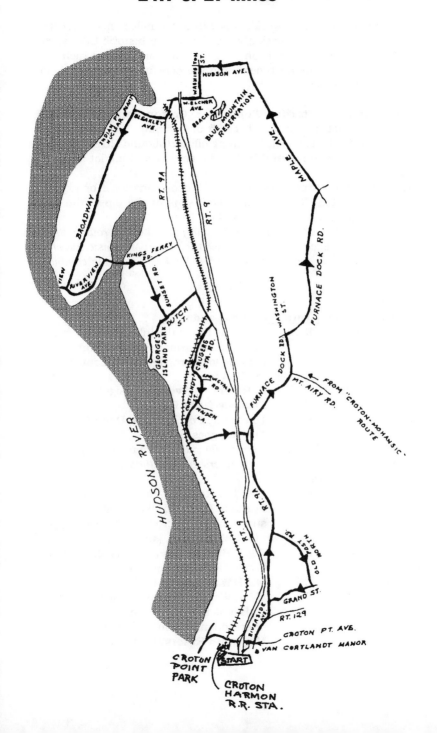

train station, you can ride an extra 2.4 miles, first over the narrow viaduct that gives a good view of the historic train yards at Croton-Harmon, then on into Croton Point Park, which has still more fabulous river views and the benefit of a cool breeze on a hot summer's day.

Directions to Starting Point: The **Croton-Harmon Railroad Station** is located off Rt. 9, north of Ossining. Take the Croton Point Ave. exit. Turn left if coming off northbound Rt. 9 and right if coming off southbound Rt. 9. The station parking lot is on the left.

Metro-North Directions: Take a Hudson Line local or express train to Croton-Harmon. The ride begins at the top of the road exiting from the station parking lot.

Note: Cyclists wishing a longer ride may combine this route with the Croton-Mohansic ride (page 78). See the Croton-Mohansic cue sheet and description for information on a 54.4 or 56.8-mile combined route.

Pt. to Point	Cume	Turn	Street/Landmark
0.0	0.0	R	From the top of the hill at the exit from the Croton-Harmon Railroad Station parking lot, turn **right** onto **Croton Point Ave.**
0.2	0.2	L	**S. Riverside Ave.** (T; no sign)
3.3	3.5	R	**Furnace Dock Rd.**
0.8	4.3	L	To continue on **Furnace Dock Rd.** (Mt. Airy Rd. goes right)

Joint Croton route comes in here; for riders coming from the Croton-Mohansic route, the numbers in parentheses represent your cumulative mileage

0.3	4.6	R	*(34.3)* At stop sign, to continue on **Furnace Dock Rd.** Washington St. goes straight. Do not cross steel deck bridge
2.5	7.1	L	*(36.8)* **Maple Ave.** (stop sign)
2.5	9.6	L	*(39.3)* **Hudson Ave.** (turn is after Dean Ferris Florist, on right)
0.8	10.4	L	*(40.1)* **Washington St.**
1.0	11.4	R	*(41.1)* **Welcher Ave.** (stop sign; Ferony's Market is in front of you at this intersection). If you wish to go into **Blue Mountain Reservation**, turn **left** here

Pt. to Point	Cume	Turn	Street/Landmark
			instead. Bear right past the entrance station to go to the **beach**, generally open weekends only and possibly only to those with Westchester park pass
0.3	11.7	L	_(41.4)_ **Rt. 9A** (traffic light after Rt. 9 underpass; sign for Indian Point)
0.4	12.1	R	_(41.8)_ **Bleakley Ave.** (toward Indian Point)
0.4	12.5	L	_(42.2)_ **Broadway** (traffic light). Go **straight** here for the **energy exhibit** at Indian Point
1.7	14.2	R	_(43.9)_ **Riverview Ave.** (T; no sign)
0.1	14.3		_(44.0)_ Enjoy the view by the end of **Riverview Ave.**, then go back the way you came. Go **straight** on Riverview Ave. (do not turn left on Broadway)
0.6	14.9	R	_(44.6)_ **Kings Ferry Rd.** (T)
0.5	15.4	R	_(45.1)_ **Sunset Rd.**
0.9	16.3	R	_(46.0)_ **Dutch St.** (T). Enter **Georges Island Park**
0.6	16.9		_(46.6)_ **U-turn** by boat launching ramp in park and ride back the way you came (picnic tables available by river)
0.6	17.5	S	_(47.2)_ **Dutch St.** (stop sign; Sunset Rd. goes left)
0.6	18.1	R	_(47.8)_ **Rt. 9A** (T)
0.6	18.7	R	_(48.4)_ **Crugers Station Rd.** (name changes to **Cortlandt St.**)
0.7	19.4	BR	_(49.1)_ At fork, to continue on **Cortlandt St.** (Springvale Rd. goes left)
0.3	19.7	BR	_(49.4)_ At fork (no sign). Cross a stream immediately
0.4	20.1	L	_(49.8)_ At T (no sign; tracks and river close at hand on your right)
0.8	20.9	R	_(50.6)_ **Old Albany Post Rd.** (T)
0.0	20.9	R	_(50.6)_ **Rt. 9A** (stop sign)
1.4	22.3	L	_(52.0)_ **Old Post Rd. North**
0.9	23.2	R	_(52.9)_ **Grand St.** (no street sign; turn is just past St. Augustine's church, which is on your right)
0.5	23.7	L	_(53.4)_ **Riverside Ave.** (T)
0.8	24.5	R	_(54.2)_ **Croton Point Ave.** (toward railroad station). Go **straight** if you wish

Pt. to Point	Cume	Turn	Street/Landmark
			to visit **Van Cortlandt Manor**
0.2	24.7		*(54.4)* **Croton-Harmon Railroad Station** parking lot on left. You may end route here, or continue straight and cross one-lane viaduct over railroad yards. Wait for long traffic light to turn green, so you don't meet up with oncoming traffic on skinny viaduct!
0.5	25.2	BR	*(54.9)* Toward **Croton Point Park**
0.7	25.9		*(55.6)* Picnic area by the river. Return the way you came in
1.0	26.9	S	*(56.6)* At traffic light to cross viaduct over railroad yards
0.2	27.1	R	*(56.8)* Into **Croton-Harmon Railroad Station** parking lot. End of route

PEEKSKILL HOLLOW RIDE - 35.6 MILES

Terrain: Gently rolling in the "hollows" with some larger climbs in between.
Traffic: Light to none, except moderate near Peekskill and on Rt. 301
Road Conditions: Good. One small section of unpaved road (Horton Brook Rd.)
Points of Interest: Cycling lightly travelled "hollows" (river valleys) in backwoods Putnam County; **Clarence Fahnestock Park** (beach, picnic area); **Sprout Brook Park** (beach, water slide).

Despite the growth of New York's outer suburbs, much of Putnam County remains quiet and lightly populated. This is partly because of geography — southwestern Putnam is a land of deep stream valleys (hollows) and few roads. This road travels long distances alongside Peekskill Hollow and Canopus creeks, enabling you to enjoy this intimate countryside with few big climbs.

Start on the edge of Peekskill and head to Putnam Valley, a growing settlement on the Westchester-Putnam county line. The turn onto Peekskill Hollow Rd. will be your last direction change for 12 miles. Every four miles or so you'll pass a tiny crossroads settlement with a gas station and general store. In between there are woods, small homes and farms and views of the hills that rise steeply out of the hollow.

Ride up Rt. 301 into the heart of Clarence Fahnestock State Park. A fine beach on Canopus Lake will cool you off, and shady picnic groves are also available.

Return to Peekskill by following Canopus Creek. This is a very remote area where many of the roads were only recently paved and still very lightly travelled. Near the end of the route you will pass Sprout Brook Park, which has the area's only water slide and a very nice lake beach.

Directions to Starting Point: Hampton Oaks IGA Supermarket Shopping Center is located on North Division St. in Peekskill. Take either Rt. 9 or the Taconic Pkwy. to Bear Mountain Pkwy., exit at Division St. and turn left. The shopping center will be on the right in less than half a mile.

PEEKSKILL HOLLOW RIDE
35.6 Miles

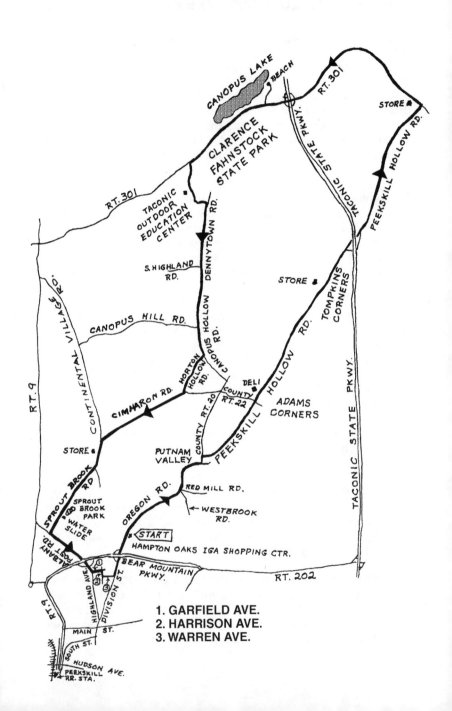

1. GARFIELD AVE.
2. HARRISON AVE.
3. WARREN AVE.

Metro-North Directions: (2 miles each way from station to start of ride): Take a Hudson Line train to Peekskill (you may have to change trains at Croton-Harmon). Turn left (north) out of the station, then make the first right onto Hudson Ave. Go under Rt. 9, then make the first left onto unmarked South St. (toward Jan Peek Square). At the T, go left onto South Division St. Bear right at the monument to continue on North Division St. and on up to the starting point. Cyclists should note that the route from the Peekskill station does not go through the nicest of neighborhoods, and should plan to cycle in pairs and be back at the station before dark.

Pt. to Point	Cume	Turn	Street/Landmark
0.0	0.0	R	Exit parking lot of Hampton Oaks IGA Supermarket Shopping Center and turn right onto **N. Division St.** Road changes name to **Oregon Rd.**
2.1	2.1	BL	At traffic light to continue on **Oregon Rd.** Red Mill Rd. and Westbrook Rd. go right
0.7	2.8	L	At traffic light (no signs; Old Oregon Medical Center is on the right)
0.1	2.9	R	At traffic light onto **Peekskill Hollow Rd.** (no sign) toward Adams Corners, Tompkins Corners and Taconic Pkwy.
2.5	5.4	S	At traffic light. Adams Corner deli on left
4.0	9.4		Tompkins Corner store on left
1.1	10.5	S	Go under Taconic State Pkwy.
4.0	14.5	L	**Rt. 301** (T). Deli on left immediately after turn
5.3	19.8	S	Go over Taconic State Pkwy.
0.3	20.1		Turn **right** for **Canopus Lake Beach Area**. After visiting beach, return to Rt. 301 and turn right
3.3	23.4	L	**Dennytown Rd.** If you start heading down a long, steep hill you've gone too far
0.7	24.1	R	At T
1.9	26.0	S	S. Highland Rd. goes right
1.3	27.3	S	Name changes to **Canopus Hollow Rd.** Canopus Hill Rd. goes right
0.5	27.8	R	**Horton Hollow Rd.** Becomes dirt

Pt. to Point	Cume	Turn	Street/Landmark
0.9	28.7	R	**Cimmaron Rd.** (T; paved road)
2.4	31.1	BL	**Continental Village Rd.** Store on right after turn
0.6	31.7	R	**Sprout Brook Rd.**
1.7	33.4		**Sprout Brook Park** (lake beach open to public; water slide) on left
0.6	34.0	L	**Albany Post Rd.** (T). Road changes name to **Highland Ave.**
0.7	34.7	L	**Garfield Ave.**
0.1	34.8	R	**Harrison Ave.**
0.1	34.9	L	**Warren Ave.**
0.1	35.0	L	**Division St.** (T; no sign)
0.6	35.6	R	Into parking area of **Hampton Oaks IGA Supermarket Shopping Center**. End of route

CROTON AQUEDUCT (ATB RIDE) - 10.0 MILES

Terrain: Flat on the aqueduct. Hilly getting up to the path and heading down to Ossining.
Traffic: The path is popular with joggers, but not overly so. One road stretch is on busy Rt. 9, but otherwise the road stretches are on quiet local streets.
Path Conditions: Excellent and hard-packed, although often skinny single-track (in a wide grassy right-of-way).
Points of Interest: Croton Dam and pleasant woods along the way.

Much of the land above the Croton Aqueduct, the original pipe bringing water down to New York City from the "countryside" of Northern Westchester, is now owned by the State of New York and makes for a pleasant, flat ATB jaunt. After-work exercisers can zip the six-mile roundtrip of aqueduct path north of Ossining and not touch fat tire to pavement.

The section described in this route is particularly agreeable because it goes through the pretty Croton Gorge area and is mostly deep in the woods, offering few signs of nearby civilization. In addition, cyclists using Metro-North can make it a one-way ride, pedaling up from the Croton-Harmon station and returning via the Ossining station.

The path starts at Croton Gorge Park, under the majestic Croton Dam. After a short climb, settle in to fast, flat cycling. Often a single skinny flat track, worn as smooth and hard as a paved road, goes down the center of the wide, grassy right of way, and the cyclist can zoom along with the old trees high above and an occasional vista of the Hudson River off to the west. Periodically one passes the old stone access towers that remind you that there is an aqueduct underneath.

At Route 9A near the northern border of Ossining a General Electric facility is built atop the aqueduct, and cyclists have to exit onto local streets which are ferociously hilly -- that granny chain ring comes in handy here. A deli is available at the bottom of one steep hill to refresh the hungry or thirsty rider. Then it's off into Ossining, first on busy Route 9, then back onto a separate path that goes past a historic mansion and ends at an Ossining

CROTON AQUEDUCT (ATB RIDE)
10.0 Miles

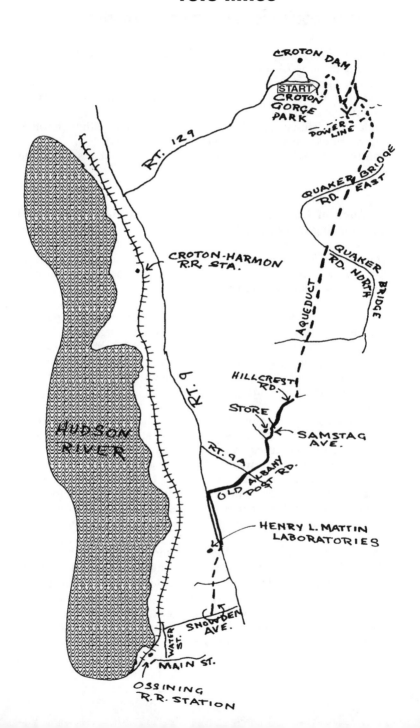

city street. Riders not heading to the train station turn around here and retrace their steps.

Directions To Starting Point: Croton Gorge Park is off Rt. 129, about 3 miles east of Rt. 9. Proceed to farthest parking lot, near restrooms (water fountain available).

Metro-North Directions: (2.9 miles to start of route). Take a Hudson Line local or express to Croton-Harmon. Follow the cue sheet of the Croton-Mohansic route (page 80) to Mile 2.9. Keep going past the foot of the dam to the farthest parking lot, near restrooms (water fountain available). Train cyclists may return via Ossining for a total ride mileage of 8.8 miles (path U-turn point is 0.7 miles from Ossining station). Follow directions at Mile 5.2 of cue sheet below.

Pt. to Point	Cume	Turn	Street/Landmark
0.0	0.0		Start on wide path near playground that first heads toward dam then curves to the south
0.2	0.2	R	At fork, taking lower path
0.3	0.5		Go under power line
0.1	0.6	SL	Climb alongside power line. Do not go straight—goes into private property
0.1	0.7	R	At top of hill, onto **aqueduct path**
0.6	1.3	S	Cross Quaker Bridge Road East
0.5	1.8	S	Cross Quaker Bridge Road North
0.5	2.3		Entering Croton Gorge Unique Area. Look for fine view of Hudson on right shortly after that
0.6	2.9	S	Another road crossing, after barrier and access tower
0.3	3.2	R	At road, where GE Property is ahead of you
0.0	3.2	S	**Hillcrest Ave.** Steep uphill, followed by steep downhill
0.3	3.5	L	**Samstag Ave.** (stop sign at bottom of hill)
0.0	3.5	L	**Old Albany Post Rd.** (stop sign). Deli on right at corner. Go downhill
0.4	3.9	L	**S. Highland Ave. (Rt. 9)** (traffic light)
0.6	4.5	R	At bus stop at top of hill. Look for sign: **"Old Croton Trailway State Park"**. Walk around barrier and enter trail

Pt. to Point	Cume	Turn	Street/Landmark
0.1	4.6		Ride behind office building and in front of grand old house that was the original headquarters for Henry L. Mattin laboratories. Look for blaze on tree. Cross road and continue on path
0.3	4.9	S	Cross road
0.3	5.2		Path ends at Snowden Ave. in Ossining. If you are riding to the Ossining railroad station, turn **right** onto **Snowden Ave.**, passing the fire station and going straight at all stop signs. In 0.5 miles, turn **left** onto **Water Street**. Turn right in 0.2 miles onto **Main St.**, which takes you directly to the train station. **U-turn** if you are returning to Croton Gorge Park
0.6	5.8	L	**Rt. 9 North**
0.4	6.2	R	Toward **Quaker Bridge Rd.** (exit before traffic light)
0.1	6.3	R	At stop sign
0.3	6.6	R	**Samstag Ave.**, at stop sign. Deli at intersection
0.1	6.7	R	**Hillcrest Ave.** Climb very steep hill
0.2	6.9	S	Cross Fowler Ave. at stop sign, toward Indian Brook Treatment Plant
0.1	7.0	L	**Aqueduct path** (before brown cinderblock building on left)
2.7.	9.7	SL	Gravel path, headed downhill
0.1	9.8	R	Switchback right
0.2	10.0		Parking lot. End of route

BLUE MOUNTAIN RESERVATION (ATB RIDE) - 3.4 MILES

Terrain: Hilly on the "intermediate" paths. Still a bit hilly on the so-called "beginner" paths. Flat on the sections through ballfield and picnic area.
Traffic: A few hikers on the trails, otherwise the park is fairly empty.
Path Conditions: Eroded and rocky in many areas.
Points of Interest: Pleasant woods, ponds and streams. Swimming beach (open weekends).

Blue Mountain Reservation is the only Westchester County park open to all-terrain bicycles. The wide hiking trails are rather rocky and eroded and, at the current maintenance level, suitable for more advanced ATB riders. Beginners can do fine if they walk any section they are uncomfortable with.

The route may be expanded by heading up a number of other marked trails in the park.   Obtain a map at the entrance. Cyclists without cars can access the park via Metro-North.

A swimming beach is available on weekends only during the summer. Parking fees at press time are $2.50 for those with a county park pass and $6 for cars without. If you bike in, it's free.

Head uphill from the parking lot into "intermediate" country, and test your skills on some rather steep hills, complete with rocks and some roots. Cross an old iron bridge and cycle through the woods alongside the park's main pond. Return to the parking lot and cycle through the picnic area to the beach.

Next try out the "beginner" trails, which still have a few challenging hills but have less erosion. These paths go by a pretty stream and include a hemlock gorge.

Directions to Starting Point: Blue Mountain Reservation is in Peekskill. Exit Rt. 9 at Welcher Ave. and turn east (right from northbound Rt. 9, left from southbound Rt. 9). Go straight at stop sign at the top of the hill to enter the park. Turn left after the toll booth and proceed to the top parking lot, past the trail lodge.

BLUE MOUNTAIN RESERVATION
(ATB RIDE) 3.4 Miles

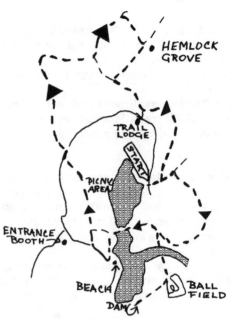

HEMLOCK GROVE

TRAIL LODGE

START

PICNIC AREA

ENTRANCE BOOTH

BEACH

DAM

BALL FIELD

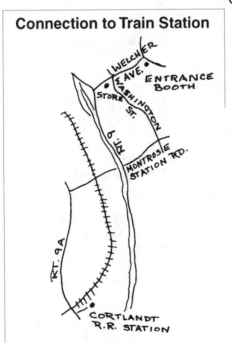

Connection to Train Station

WELCHER AVE.

ENTRANCE BOOTH

STORE

WASHINGTON ST.

RT. 9

MONTROSE STATION RD.

RT. 9A

CORTLANDT R.R. STATION

Metro-North Directions: (3.2 miles from train station to park). Take a Hudson Line train to the new Cortlandt station. Ride out the station driveway and turn right on Rt. 9A North. Proceed 1 mile and turn right on Montrose Station Road. Ride 0.8 miles to the stop sign and turn left on Washington St. Continue 0.9 miles to the stop sign at Welcher Ave., where there is a deli on the left to buy lunch. Turn right and enter the park. Ride left at the intersection after the toll booth, and head 0.5 miles to the top parking lot, where the route begins.

Pt. to Point	Cume	Turn	Street/Landmark
0.0	0.0	R	Take trail coming off parking lot opposite lake. Climb rocky uphill immediately
0.1	0.1	R	Onto trail marked with an orange checkerboard sign
0.2	0.3	S	At intersection at bottom of hairy descent, to continue on orange trail. Ride alongside stream, and continue going down hill
0.2	0.5	L	Gravel path, heading over old iron bridge
0.1	0.6	R	Ride along right side of baseball field, keeping stream to your right. Look for path entering woods, alongside stream
0.2	0.8		Turn around just past dam (path ends ahead) and return to baseball field. Go back over iron bridge, and ride on gravel path
0.4	1.2	L	Onto paved path at T, riding through picnic area by the lake
0.1	1.3	R	Beach parking area (beach on left; restrooms in picnic area or in beach)
0.1	1.4	R	Dirt path marked "Service Road/ Authorized Vehicles Only", into picnic area
0.1	1.5	BL	By big tree, with swing set in front of you
0.1	1.6	R	Paved car road
0.0	1.6	L	Onto bike trail, heading into woods
0.3	1.9	SR	At unmarked intersection. Continue on widest path
0.4	2.3	L	At junction where trail going right goes

Pt. to Point	Cume	Turn	Street/Landmark
			over small stream bridge. Continue following orange-and-white checkerboard blazes
0.2	2.5	R	Continue following orange-and-white checkerboard blazes where red-blazed path goes straight. Sign says footpath only, but park map indicates this is a bike path. Cross fragile footbridge
0.2	2.7	R	At intersection in midst of hemlock grove
0.1	2.8	L	At T intersection, following orange-and-white checkerboards. Blue trail goes right
0.1	2.9	L	Curve left back into woods and climb where you can exit trail onto car road by trail lodge
0.4	3.3	R	At T intersection. Head carefully down hill
0.1	3.4		Parking lot. End of route

RIDES STARTING IN THE LOWER HUDSON VALLEY (WEST SIDE OF RIVER)

West of the Hudson River the land rises more abruptly than it does on the Westchester side. Prominent hills and mountains, rare in Westchester, dot the landscape of Rockland County. And Bergen County has the Palisades, that huge riverside cliff that forces the cyclist to ride uphill instead of down to reach the Hudson.

Suburbia and overcrowded roads have overrun most of Bergen and much of Rockland. But thanks to the Palisades Interstate Park Commission, there is still a lot of great riding in this section, featuring woods, hills, views — and lots of history, because the Hudson Valley was a major theater of the Revolutionary War.

For readers of the first edition of *RIDE GUIDE/Hudson Valley and Sound Shore*, you will note two changes — rides originating in Bear Mountain are grouped in the Mid-Hudson Valley section because that's the direction they head, and riders wishing to stay right in New York City have their very own ride.

Around New York Harbor is a route with a major caveat — it is only enjoyable when cycled early on a Sunday morning. Then you can enjoy the mouth of the Hudson from both sides with minimal interference from automobiles. And what enjoyment you will have as you tour the Big Apple, one of the most striking cities in the world when viewed from two wheels. Starting in New Jersey's Liberty State Park, this route heads to Staten Island, includes a ride aboard the Staten Island Ferry, then hits the highlights of Manhattan from Battery to Riverside Park before crossing the George Washington Bridge back into New Jersey. The return route includes striking views of the New York skyline up close and personal, with the Hudson in the foreground.

Fort Lee-Nyack has been a favorite of cyclists from New York for decades. And now with Henry Hudson Drive, the woodsy strip of pavement under the cliff of the Palisades, open to bicycles at all times, it is even more of a pleasure. Piermont has become a tourist destination in its own right, and Nyack a few miles north has long been known for its antique shops and good restaurants. An option is given to combine with the Nyack Ride, or you can cycle back immediately via quiet suburban roads.

The **Nyack Ride** is an easy loop which features a 2.5-mile bike path along the river under Hook Mountain and only one terrible hill — rising up the side of this mountain from river level to Rockland Lake State Park. This loop passes Tappan and the Piermont Pier, and includes a side trip to a quiet swimming pool in Tallman Mountain State Park.

Saddle River-Stony Point passes rural and woodsy stretches of Bergen and Rockland en route to Stony Point. This hilly peninsula on the Hudson was the site of a successful sneak attack on the British by General "Mad Anthony" Wayne. You will not go thirsty or hungry negotiating the many climbs of this ride — the route passes a winery and innumerable country stores and delicatessens.

AROUND NEW YORK HARBOR - 41.2 MILES

Terrain: Flat to rolling, with some fairly steep hills on the New Jersey side, and a few unexpected leg-testers in Manhattan.

Traffic: This is New York City, after all, but if this loop is done at the recommended hour of early Sunday morning, the traffic is surprisingly light in Manhattan. The heaviest traffic is on the New Jersey side, especially by the Lincoln Tunnel entrance, but for the most part it's moderate.

Road Conditions: Fairly decent, considering how heavily traveled these roads are.

Points of Interest: Fantastic **views** of Manhattan, New York Harbor, the Kill van Kull, Hudson River and the George Washington Bridge; New York's financial district, midtown, Central Park and Upper West Side; **Fort Lee Historic Park**; the Weehauken spot where Alexander Hamilton lost his duel to Aaron Burr; Hoboken, hometown of baseball and Frank Sinatra; pretty campus of **Stevens Institute of Technology**.

This is a ride I've always wanted to do, ever since I rode the annual madness known as the Five Borough Bike Tour. New York City is a beautiful place to bike through — gorgeous architecture, great parks, statues, views — especially when the cyclist does not have to worry too much about traffic.

For this reason, I recommend only attempting this loop early on a Sunday or holiday morning. If you are doing the cue sheet exactly as it appears, leave Liberty State Park no later than 7:30 a.m. so you can catch the 9:00 a.m. ferry from Staten Island.

Before setting out on this loop, be sure to call the Port Authority Police at the Bayonne Bridge at 718-390-2502 to make sure that the pedestrian path is open! It was closed for construction during most of 1995. Signs forecast reopening in fall 1995, but it did not open until late spring 1996! If it is closed, you can do a modified version of the route by reversing the route from the end to Hoboken, using the PATH train to reach lower Manhattan, then cycling back to Liberty State Park, or start at Hoboken and skip Liberty State Park altogether.

A few warnings are necessary before the novice suburbanite or out-of-towner sets spoked wheel in the Big Apple: Ride on the right side of one-way roads, except 6th Avenue above 34th Street where the bike path is on the left and there is no parking lane on the right; watch for car doors opening; beware of cab drivers, who drive from one side of the road to the other without looking — you cannot predict their behavior in advance; watch for pedestrians, who ignore traffic lights and dare you to hit them; also be wary of native New York City cyclists, who also ignore traffic lights and may run down those who don't; watch for fast-moving in-line skaters, runners and cyclists in Central Park; and, believe it or not, another hazard to avoid are tourists who will stand in the road gawking at the tall buildings oblivious to oncoming bicyclists. A good strategy (except between 34th and 59th Streets) is to ride right on the line separating the parking lane with the right-most travel line, which should give you enough room to avoid car doors suddenly opening in your path. Expect to go about ten blocks between red lights, if you can achieve a steady cadence.

Bearing all that in mind, you will absolutely enjoy this loop as long as you start by 7:30 a.m. Sunday or holiday! If you are already in New York City, start the route anywhere that's convenient, or take PATH to Hoboken and begin there (that is, if the Bayonne Bridge pedestrian path is open; if it is not, start in Manhattan and at Hoboken either take PATH back to Manhattan or continue beyond Hoboken to Liberty State Park and turn around and return to Hoboken). If you're coming in by train from Westchester, pedal west several blocks from Grand Central Terminal to join the route on Ave. of the Americas (6th Ave.) in midtown Manhattan.

For drivers from the suburbs, Liberty State Park is the logical starting point. It offers the most astonishing of all the many amazing views on the New Jersey side of the Hudson, has good picnic lawns for lunch after the route, plus the additional attractions of the Liberty Science Center and/or ferries to the Statue of Liberty and Ellis Island for after the ride.

Pedaling off early in the morning from this spot, head south along undeveloped coastal swamps along roads as deserted on a Sunday morning as country roads far to the west or north. Skirt the city streets of Bayonne on an expressway with a wide shoulder that has practically no traffic early Sunday — look for military ships at the Bayonne Ocean Terminal.

Next, cross the Bayonne Bridge, one of the longest arch bridges in the world, into Staten Island. The Kill Van Kull below is one of the world's busiest shipping channels. The ride along the Staten

Island waterfront is industrial, but quiet on a Sunday morning. Pedal into the ferry terminal to catch the 9:00 a.m. boat (they leave once an hour), and enjoy a close-up view of Lady Liberty off the left side.

In 25 minutes you'll be back on land and riding under the tall towers of New York's financial district, passing right next to the city's tallest buildings, the World Trade Center. Next, pass Greenwich Village, already starting to get busy with Sunday morning art and antique markets. The Garment District in the 20's and 30's also feature antique markets.

After you pass 34th Street, you'll be forced to a "bike lane" on the left side of the road, rather difficult because chances are your mirror is on your left. Just be aware of nearby taxicabs and you'll do fine. Enjoy the sights of midtown Manhattan, including Bryant Park, New York Public Library, Rockefeller Center, Radio City Music Hall and Central Park South — there is no better way to go than two wheels.

Enter Central Park, busy with fast-moving recreationalists. Walkers, skaters and joggers are all segregated into their own lanes on the park road, but horse-drawn carriages (and their associated residue) share the bike lane!

Turn west at the Central Park lake (a restroom is very convenient to the route here at the Boat House restaurant). Exit the park by the famous Dakota Apartments, then head west through the attractive residential towers of the Upper West Side to Riverside Drive. This road is one of the most attractive in Manhattan, bordered on both sides by trees with excellent river views. There are also some challenging hills. Sights along the way include Riverside Church and Grant's Tomb, a favorite destination of our cycling ancestors in the gay '90s (1890s, that is!).

At 165th Street you will climb into the Washington Heights neighborhood, go under the quadruple pedestrian skybridges of Columbia Presbyterian Hospital, and start across the George Washington Bridge into New Jersey. From the bridge it's a steep, hairy descent down the Palisades to Edgewater. Traffic is a bit busy in this area, as River Road is the only major road under the cliffs. The area along the river used to be industrial and full of railyards but is developing into residential and retail, with many Japanese-owned businesses serving the large Asian population of this part of Bergen County.

AROUND NEW YORK HARBOR
41.2 Miles

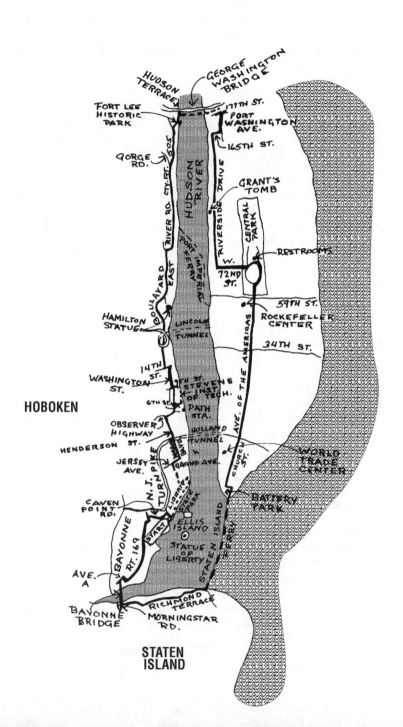

Climb back to clifftop at West New York. In Weehauken, across from the towers of midtown Manhattan, a small bust of Alexander Hamilton marks the spot where he lost his duel with Aaron Burr.

A downhill takes you by the entrance to the Lincoln Tunnel, easily the hairiest traffic of the route. Then it's over a viaduct into Hoboken, whose entrance sign proclaims it the birthplace of baseball and Frank Sinatra. The city has a large yuppie population of ex-Manhattanites and block after block of attractive brownstones.

The route climbs some narrow side streets to allow you to tour the campus of Stevens Institute of Technology, one of the most attractive college campuses in the New York area. You'll have to walk your bike on some of the campus paths, but it's worth the detour.

Next pass the Hoboken railroad terminal, where those who began the route in Manhattan can return via the PATH train (open to bikes on weekends). The route to Liberty State Park goes through a less-than-desirable section of Jersey City — it is recommended that it be ridden in pairs.

Finally, find the bike path back into Liberty State Park at an unlikely industrial-looking dead-end road, and enjoy the breathtaking views of the financial district and the Statue of Liberty as you ride along the mile-long riverfront promenade.

Directions to Starting Point: Liberty State Park is off Exit 14B of the New Jersey Turnpike Northeast Extension, not far from the Holland Tunnel. Turn left after paying the toll. As you enter the park, go straight ahead toward the park office (not toward the Science Center or Statue of Liberty ferries). Park in the first parking lot after the Boat Launching area.

Pt. to Point	Cume	Turn	Street/Landmark
0.0	0.0	L	Exit parking lot and turn **left** toward **park exit.**
0.3	0.3	L	Toward New Jersey Turnpike
0.1	0.4	L	At traffic light, toward Port Liberte, on unmarked **Caven Point Rd.**
1.0	1.4	S	At first intersection, keeping ballfield on left and turnpike on right

Pt. to Point	Cume	Turn	Street/Landmark
0.4	1.8	L	At next intersection, following signs for New Jersey Turnpike (even though you are turning away from the turnpike)
0.1	1.9	R	Toward New Jersey Turnpike. You are on **Rt. 169 South**. Stay on the wide shoulder and cross railroad tracks
1.0	2.9		Use caution crossing bumpy railroad crossing
0.7	3.6		Watch out for another railroad crossing that comes at a funny angle
0.1	3.7	S	At traffic light by Bayonne Military Ocean Terminal, continuing on **Rt. 169 South**
1.8	5.5		Use caution as shoulder disappears for viaduct over railroad
0.5	6.0		Take **Ave. A exit**
0.0	6.0	L	At stop sign at end of ramp, onto **Ave. A**
0.2	6.2	L	At traffic light, onto **W. 4th St.**
0.0	6.2	R	**Bayonne Bridge path** (climb stairs)
1.3	7.5		Exit on Staten Island side onto **Morningstar Road**, just path toll booths (bikes don't pay)
0.1	7.6	R	**Morningstar Road** (stop sign at end of exit ramp)
0.4	8.0	R	**Richmond Terrace** (T)
1.0	9.0	L	To continue on **Richmond Terrace**
1.1	10.1	L	Curve left to continue on **Richmond Terrace**, following sign for Snug Harbor
1.1	11.2	L	Into **Ferry Terminal** to catch boat for Manhattan (use car entrance onto lower level of ferry)
0.0	11.2		Exit Ferry Terminal and aim for small red building under skyscrapers, the **Shrine of Elizabeth Ann Seton**
0.2	11.4	BL	At traffic light, onto **State Street**
0.0	11.4	L	To continue around Battery Park (which is on your left)
0.0	11.4	R	First right turn onto **Greenwich Street** which becomes **Trinity Place.** Pass Battery Park Garage on left
0.3	11.7		Back of **Trinity Church** on right at corner of Rector St.
0.2	11.9	S	Road becomes **Church Street** as you

Pt. to Point	Cume	Turn	Street/Landmark
			pass the **World Trade Center** on your left
0.7	12.6	L	Curve left after crossing Franklin St. onto **Ave. of the Americas (6th Ave.)**. Do not take any angled street coming off Ave. of the Americas
0.2	12.8	S	Carefully cross Canal Street, which is very wide here, and continue on Ave. of the Americas. A taxi garage will be on your right after the intersection
2.1	14.9	S	Cross Broadway and 34th St. at Herald Square and cross to left side of road to use **bike lane** (parking is now prohibited on the right side and you don't want to be in a travel lane with cars unless you are a professional bike messenger!)
0.4	15.3		**Bryant Park** and rear of **New York Public Library** on right (between 40th and 42nd Streets)
0.6	15.9		**Rockefeller Center** on left at 49th St. **Radio City Music Hall** on right at 51st Street
0.3	16.2	S	Cross 59th Street and enter **Central Park** on **Center Drive** (closed to cars), Careful merging into main park loop -- stay in the bike lanes
0.8	17.0	BL	At fork, heading toward **West 72nd St.** Note: If you need a **restroom**, continue **straight** at the fork for 0.1 miles to **Boathouse Restaurant** on left, which has convenient bike-in restrooms just off the park loop road. Then return to the fork headed west
0.1	17.1		Pull off to the right side of the road to admire the amazing view of the **fountain and lake**
0.2	17.3		Merge onto main park loop, cross to right side, and then take the right fork toward **West 72nd St.**
0.3	17.6	S	Carefully cross Central Park West at the **Dakota Apartments** onto **W. 72nd St.**
0.5	18.1	R	**Riverside Dr.** (just before Henry Hudson Pkwy. entrance)

Pt. to Point	Cume	Turn	Street/Landmark
0.9	19.0		**Soldiers and Sailors Monument** on left at 88th Street
1.6	20.6		**Riverside Church** on right at 120th St.
0.1	20.7		**Grant's Tomb** on left
0.2	20.9		Cross viaduct with fabulous views of George Washington Bridge and Hudson River
1.4	22.3		Enter a shorter viaduct with another great bridge view
0.6	22.9	R	**165th St**. Climb short, steep hill
0.1	23.0	L	**Fort Washington Ave**. Go under pedestrian skyways of Columbia Presbyterian Hospital
0.6	23.6	L	**W. 177th St**. (one block before bridge highway overpass)
0.1	23.7	R	**Cabrini Blvd.** (two blocks from last turn)
0.1	23.8	L	Cross street and head toward **George Washington Bridge bikepath** and pedestrian walkway. Use caution (slow) going around the two towers
1.3	25.1	L	**Hudson Terrace**, at end of path
0.1	25.2		**Fort Lee Historic Park on left**. Good picnic stop; restrooms available. Lock your bike near entrance booth as bikes are not allowed in park
0.1	25.3	BL	At stop sign, onto busy road **(River Rd./County Rt. 505)** heading down very steep hill toward river. Control your speed!
3.1	28.4	S	**River Road** (where Old River Road forks to the right)
0.4	28.8	S	Continue straight where Gorge Road goes off right
1.3	30.1		Just past Port Imperial Ferry (an alternate for the tired to sail back to Manhattan), begin 3/4-mile climb
0.6	30.7	L	At traffic light, onto **Boulevard East**. Enjoy gorgeous views toward Manhattan all along this road (did you bring your binoculars?)
1.2	31.9		Where road curves right, away from river, take a **side trip** on the **small road going along the river** to see the **statue**

Pt. to Point	Cume	Turn	Street/Landmark
			of Alexander Hamilton, on the left. Then return to **Boulevard East**
0.1	32.0		Curve left at traffic light, following **Boulevard East** and signs for Stevens
0.4	32.4	S	Go under Lincoln Tunnel viaduct. Watch for heavy traffic merging from right, joining you, then cutting in front of you to head toward tunnel
0.6	33.0	S	**Park Ave.** Go onto viaduct headed toward Hoboken. Viaduct has good shoulder, but watch for double-width storm drains at beginning and end of viaduct
0.4	33.4	L	**14th St.** (traffic light)
0.2	33.6	R	**Washington St.** Enjoy central Hoboken, but watch for cars backing out of angle parking places
0.4	34.0	L	**9th St**. Follow signs toward Stevens. Climb steep hill, going straight at two stop signs
0.2	34.2	S	Enter campus of **Stevens Institute of Technology** at gate
0.2	34.4	S	Where sign says all traffic go right, walk your bike next to tall building on left (Stevens Center), and continue to walk bike downhill, parallel to Hudson River, out of campus
0.1	34.5	R	Exit campus at gate, remount your bike and turn right onto 6th St.
0.1	34.6	L	**Hudson St.**, at stop sign
0.5	35.1		If you are returning to Manhattan via PATH, turn left at Hudson Place, which takes you directly to PATH station. Otherwise, go straight. *From here to Liberty State Park, be sure to ride in pairs*
0.1	35.2	R	**Observer Highway** (T). Bumpy, busy road alongside railroad tracks
0.4	35.6	L	**Henderson St.** Watch for broken glass
0.3	35.9	S	Cross exit road from Holland Tunnel
0.1	36.0	S	Cross entrance road to Holland Tunnel. Road changes name to **Luis Munoz Marin Blvd.**

Pt. to Point	Cume	Turn	Street/Landmark
1.0	37.0	R	**Grand Ave.** (where "no outlet" street goes straight)
0.3	37.3	L	**Jersey Ave.** Head toward not-very-promising-looking dead end
0.3	37.6	S	Through sand at cul-de-sac onto **bike path** into Liberty State Park. Cross wooden bridge over old Morris Canal basin
0.1	37.7	L	At end of bridge. Ride along dirt for short distance, then onto **paved path along canal basin**
0.7	38.4	S	At tour boat dock
0.2	38.6	R	**Cobble path** toward old railroad station
0.1	38.7		Head toward **promenade** behind railroad station. If path still appears under construction, use some creativity to get there — go through railroad station and exit toward "Ferry to NY". You can get through. Path will go alongside old station shed
0.4	39.1	L	**Promenade** again parallels Hudson River
0.4	39.5	S	Pass vehicle bridge to Ellis Island (no pedestrians allowed at press time, but that is supposed to change in a few years)
1.0	40.5	R	Off cobble path directly behind Statue of Liberty, onto **paved path by water**
0.2	40.7	L	At snack bar, to continue on **paved path by water**
0.5	41.2	R	Into **parking area**. End of route

FORT LEE-NYACK - 42.6 MILES

Terrain: Hilly in spots, especially long, extended hills near and in the Palisades, but long stretches are relatively flat.
Traffic: Few cars on Henry Hudson Drive (River Drive), none on bike paths. Otherwise, moderate.
Road Conditions: Good. No dirt, not even on the bike paths.
Points of Interest: Fort Lee Historic Park (visitor's center; interpretive trails and great views of Manhattan); **Henry Hudson Drive** through **Palisades Interstate Park**; views from the **Palisades** and **Tallman Mountain**; uncrowded swimming pool at Tallman **Mountain State Park**; **Nyack** shops and restaurants; **Washington's Headquarters** and town green in **Tappan; George Washington Bridge** bike path.

Henry Hudson Drive is an old scenic auto road which provides dramatic views of the metropolis across the river while you cycle through the near wilderness of Palisades Interstate Park. Thanks to the efforts of the Bicycle Touring Club of North Jersey and others, this road is now open to multi-speed bicycles with wheels at least 24 inches in diameter (this includes the readers of this guide and excludes children on BMX bikes). Few cars travel this road, and it represents almost wilderness riding within close sight of New York City.

For some bizarre reason, Fort Lee Historic Park, the starting point for this ride is *closed* to bikes! But I have it on good authority from the park police that you will not be hassled if you drive into the park with a bike on your car, as long as you walk your bike out of the park (you can use a path parallel to the entrance to the entrance road). If you are uncomfortable with this, there is ample street parking on Hudson Terrace and surrounding streets—many cyclists park near here to begin their rides on Hudson Valley Drive.

Rt. 9W, which you get to when you climb back out of Palisades Interstate Park, is a major thoroughfare for cyclists headed north out of New York City (most of the cars are on the nearby Palisades Interstate Pkwy., leaving Rt. 9W relatively car-free). Divert off 9W in New York State to ride into Tallman Mountain State Park. There's a nice pool where you can cool off in the summer for a very reasonable admission fee.

FORT LEE-NYACK
42.6 Miles

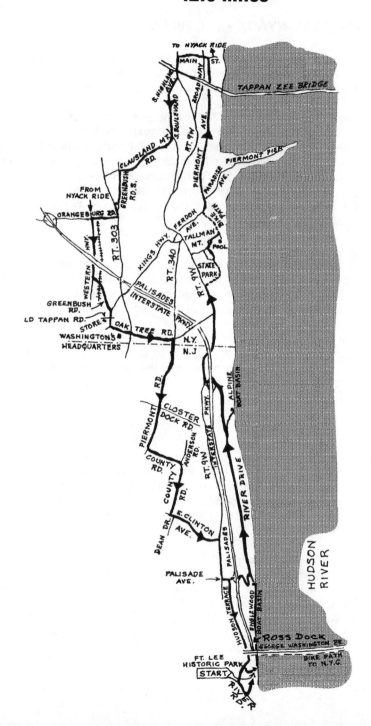

Head up toward the wide Tappan Zee through pretty Piermont (a side trip allows you to head out the pier that Piermont is named for). Grand View, a strip of large homes overlooking the Hudson, is appropriately named. In Nyack, check out the many antique shops. Perhaps carry your lunch a little further; the hills of Blauvelt State Park must be crossed, and the town green in Tappan is a good spot to rest after these hills.

Tappan has a green, some old buildings and a Washington's Headquarters museum. The return route is inland through wealthy Bergen County suburbs. E. Clinton Ave. is a very long up, up, up to the top of the Palisades — then it's flat or downhill back to Fort Lee. Be sure to take a spin out onto the George Washington Bridge bike path at the end of the route.

Directions to Starting Point: Fort Lee Historic Park is located just south of the George Washington Bridge. If you are driving across the bridge, use the upper level, exit at Hudson Terrace and turn right. The park entrance is a left turn just after going under the bridge highway. From New Jersey, use the local lanes and exit at Fort Lee (immediately before bridge tollbooths). Turn left, drive to where the road ends at Hudson Terrace, then turn right, and immediately turn left into the park. There is a fee for parking if you arrive after 9 a.m. Cyclists from New York City may ride across the bridge (see Around New York Harbor cue sheet Miles 22.9 - 23.8 for exact approach from Riverside Drive) and turn left on Hudson Terrace.

Note: This route may be combined with the Nyack Ride (page 118) for a 53.4-mile route. At Mile 18.5, in Nyack, turn right onto Main St., then left onto Gedney St., which is the beginning of the Nyack Ride. At Mile 19.8 of the Nyack Ride, rejoin the Fort Lee-Nyack route at Mile 25.8.

Pt. to Point	Cume	Turn	Street/Landmark
0.0	0.0		Walk your bike down path paralleling exit road of Fort Lee Historic Park
0.1	0.1	L	**Hudson Terrace** (T)
0.1	0.2	BL	At stop sign onto **River Rd. (County Rt. 505)** heading downhill toward river
0.1	0.3	L	**Henry Hudson Dr.** (also called **River Dr.**) heading into Palisades Park.
1.0	1.3		At circle, do not go downhill toward Ross Dock but continue around circle, turn **right** and head north on **River Rd.**

Pt. To Point	Cume	Turn	Street/Landmark
1.4	2.7	L	Do not go down to Englewood Boat Basin, but continue north on **River Dr.**, climbing away from river
0.4	3.1	S	Sharp left goes up hill to Englewood (bicycles are prohibited)
4.3	7.4		At traffic circle with little log cabin in the middle, do not head down toward river (and Alpine Boat Basin), but continue around circle and turn **right** to continue on **River Dr.** (no signs!). You will be climbing again
1.0	8.4	BL	At Palisades Interstate Pkwy. southbound entrance, following signs for Rt. 9W. Go under parkway
0.3	8.7	R	At traffic light onto **Rt. 9W North**
4.5	13.2		Entering New York State
1.1	14.3	R	Onto **bike path** (just past old-fashioned looking Gulf Station with Oasis Grill on right, and not far past traffic light in Palisades)
1.3	15.6	R	At end of bike path (T)
0.2	15.8	R	At T; follow **bike route** signs
0.1	15.9	R	At traffic circle toward **pool** (following bike route signs)
0.1	16.0	L	To continue on **bike path**. Turn **sharp right** to go to Tallman Mountain **pool**
0.5	16.5	R	At end of path. Cross steel deck bridge onto **Piermont Ave.**
0.1	16.6		Turn right onto **Paradise Ave.** for side trip to Piermont Pier
3.7	20.3	L	**Main St.**, downtown Nyack (T). *Turn **right** here to join Nyack Ride (page 120). Go to **Gedney St.** and turn **left**, then pick up Nyack Ride at the beginning of its cue sheet*
0.7	21.0	L	**Rt. 9W** (traffic light at crest of hill)
0.1	21.1	BR	After crossing New York Thruway onto **S. Highland Ave.** (sign for Nyack College)
0.3	21.4	S	Street name changes to **South Boulevard**
0.9	22.3	S	At unmarked intersection. Street name changes to **Clausland Mtn. Rd.**

Pt. to Point	Cume	Turn	Street/Landmark
2.5	24.8	L	**Greenbush Rd. South**
0.7	25.5	R	Toward **Rt. 303**
0.0	25.5	L	**Rt. 303 South** (traffic light)
0.3	25.8	R	**Orangeburg Rd.** (traffic light)
0.2	26.0	L	**Western Highway** (first traffic light)
1.2	27.2	L	**Greenbush Rd.** (street sign is hidden on the left. You will cross over railroad tracks shortly after the turn)
0.4	27.6	S	At stop sign onto **Kings Highway**. The small Tappan town green is on your right *(Riders from the Nyack Ride, rejoin here)*
0.1	27.7	S	At the traffic light, crossing Old Tappan Rd.
0.1	27.8	L	**Oak Tree Rd.**
0.2	28.0		**George Washington's Headquarters museum** on right
0.2	28.2	S	Cross Rt. 303
0.9	29.1	R	**Rt. 340**
0.4	29.5		Name changes to **Piermont Rd.** at New Jersey border
3.5	33.0	S	Cross Closter Dock Rd.
0.8	33.8	L	Curve **left** onto **County Rd. (Rt. 501 South)**. Deli on right shortly before the turn
0.6	34.4	R	Curve **right** to continue on **Rt. 501 South** (Anderson Rd. goes left)
1.0	35.4		Historic **Captain John Huyler** house on left
1.0	36.4	L	At traffic light to continue on **Rt. 501 South**
0.1	36.5	S	At blinking red light onto **E. Clinton Ave. (County Rt. 72)** (Dean Dr. goes right)
2.0	38.5	R	**Rt. 9W South** (T)
1.8	40.3	L	**Palisades Ave.** (traffic light)
0.1	40.4	R	**Hudson Terrace**
2.0	42.4		**George Washington Bridge** bike path goes left (after going under bridge highway). Worth a side trip
0.1	42.5	L	Into **Fort Lee Historic Park.** Walk bike up path (stairway) before entrance road
0.1	42.6		**Visitor's Center** (end of route)

NYACK RIDE - 26.3 MILES

Terrain: Mostly rolling hills inland and flat along the Hudson River. There is one killer ascent from the river to Rockland Lake State Park.

Traffic: Light to moderate, except heavier near Congers and West Nyack. No traffic at all along the Hudson River bike path north of Nyack!

Road Conditions: Pretty good, with occasional bumpy spots. The 2 1/2 mile bike path is unpaved, but very smooth and rock-free. Many roads have no shoulders.

Points of Interest: Nyack shops and restaurants; Hudson River bike path in **Nyack State Park; Rockland Lake State Park** (swimming and boating); historic **Tappan**; the **Piermont Pier**; swimming at **Tallman Mountain State Park**.

Nyack **is a scenic** and interesting Hudson River town and the perfect place to begin and end this fairly easy tour of southeastern Rockland County. Its antique shops and good eateries attract large crowds every weekend.

The route gets you away from the crowds quickly, heading north along Broadway into posh Upper Nyack. Beautiful homes grace this broad boulevard, and little traffic bothers cyclists. The reason for the light traffic looms ahead in the form of Hook Mountain: Cars must turn around at Nyack State Park while bikes may continue under the mountain along the river, with fine views south to the Tappan Zee and across to Sing Sing Prison.

You may wish to walk the long, very steep hill up from the river. A quick dip in the pool at Rockland Lake State Park may be in order on a hot day, but it is recommended you swim at the smaller, much less crowded pool at Tallman Mountain State Park near the end of the ride.

Cycling inland, you pass Congers, where food is available. Next, descend to and across Lake DeForest. The route then heads south to historic Tappan, where an exploring cyclist can find several historic houses and a pleasant town green.

In a couple of miles you are back on the Hudson. A bike path leads to the aforementioned pool at Tallman Mountain, where

NYACK RIDE
26.3 Miles

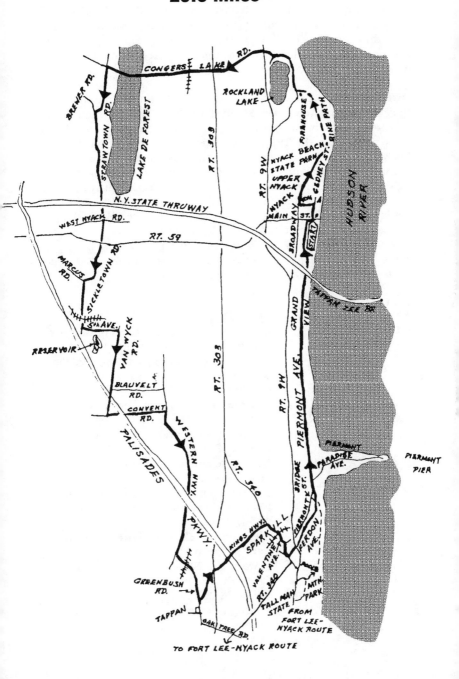

admission is very reasonable. Riders may wish to take an additional detour to the Piermont Pier. An unpaved road leads onto the pier, formerly a railroad-ferry terminal, now a parklike peninsula that juts out a full mile into the river. The final part of the route passes more fine homes in the appropriately named village of Grand View before returning to Nyack.

Directions to Starting Point: The route begins at the intersection of **Gedney and Main St.** in downtown Nyack, which is the last turn off Main St. before it reaches the Hudson River. If you are driving from the Tappan Zee Bridge, use Exit 11 off the New York Thruway. Go straight at the end of the ramp, proceed to the second light (Midland Ave.) and turn right. Main St. is the first light; turn left. From the southbound New York Thruway, take Exit 11 and turn left at the end of the ramp. This is Rt. 59, which leads you directly onto Main St. after you cross Rt. 9W. Parking is available on the street and in nearby municipal lots.

Note: You may easily combine this ride with the Fort Lee-Nyack route (page 113) for a 53.4-mile trek. See the Fort Lee-Nyack write-up and cue sheet for directions.

Pt. to Point	Cume	Turn	Street/Landmark
0.0	0.0		Start ride at the intersection of **Gedney St.** and **Main St.** in downtown Nyack. Ride north on **Gedney St.** (the Hudson River will be on your right)
0.2	0.2	L	**4th Ave.**
0.2	0.4	R	**N. Broadway** (stop sign; no street sign)
1.7	2.1	R	Into **Nyack State Park**. Go down the hill. (Restrooms and water on left at bottom of hill)
0.3	2.4	S	Onto **bike route**. Near end of bike path bear **left** at fork
2.5	4.9		Emerge from bike path and climb large hill away from river
0.4	5.3	R	At fork (no sign). Fork is just past firehouse on left. **Rockland Lake State Park** will be on your left
1.0	6.3	R	Toward **Rt. 9W**
0.1	6.4	S	Cross Rt. 9W onto **Lake Rd.**
0.3	6.7	S	Cross Rt. 303
0.5	7.2	S	Through Congers where there are two delicatessens

Pt. to Point	Cume	Turn	Street/Landmark
0.2	7.4	S	Cross Kings Highway
1.3	8.7	L	**Strawtown Rd.** (First turn past lake)
2.3	11.0	L	At T and stop sign to continue on **Strawtown Rd.** (Brewer Rd. goes right)
1.6	12.6	S	At stop sign to continue on **Strawtown Rd.**
0.7	13.3	S	Cross W. Nyack Rd. at traffic light onto **Sickletown Rd.**
1.0	14.3	L	To continue on **Sickletown Rd.** (Marcus Rd. goes right)
0.8	15.1	L	**5th Ave.** (immediately after tunnel)
0.5	15.6	R	**Van Wyck Rd.** (T)
0.9	16.5	L	**Convent Rd.** (T)
0.9	17.4	R	**Western Highway South** (T)
2.0	19.4	BL	**Greenbush Rd.** (Street sign is hidden on the left. You will go over a railroad crossing shortly after the turn)
0.4	19.8	SL	**Kings Highway** (stop sign). **Bear right** to go into **Tappan** (town green; old houses). *Riders going to Fort Lee: Continue at Mile 25.8 of Fort Lee-Nyack ride*
0.6	20.4	S	Cross Rt. 303
0.9	21.3	BR	**Rt. 340** (yield sign)
0.2	21.5	S	Cross railroad tracks at traffic light
0.1	21.6	R	**Valentine Ave.**
0.0	21.6	BL	Continue on **Rt. 340**
0.1	21.7	L	**Ferdon Ave.** (toward Piermont)
0.8	22.5		Turn **right** across from Bridge St. (on left) for 1/2-mile bike path to **swimming pool** at Tallman Mountain State Park
0.0	22.5	L	Over bridge onto **Piermont Ave.** (After crossing bridge turn **right** onto **Paradise Ave.** for side trip to Piermont Pier)
3.7	26.2	R	**Main St.** (T)
0.1	26.3		Intersection of **Main and Gedney St.** in downtown Nyack. End of route

SADDLE RIVER-STONY POINT - 45.9 MILES

Terrain: Easy going in New Jersey and near Grassy Point. Otherwise, rolling to downright hilly.
Traffic: Mostly light, with a few brief moderate sections.
Road Conditions: Mostly good, but some rough pavement, especially on South Mountain Rd.
Points of Interest: High Tor Winery and Vineyard; Stony Point State Historic Park (picnic areas, visitor's center, historic lighthouse, fabulous views of hills and Hudson River)

Most people think of Storm King, Crow's Nest and the other mountains near West Point when they think of the Hudson Highlands immortalized by painters from the Hudson River School. The southern extremity of that range of hills is in northern Rockland County, and this route gives you great views of those higher mountains while riding over the "lower" mountains.

Start in Saddle River, a still-rural (in appearance) part of Bergen County famous as the home of the late President Nixon. Head north on the back roads of Monsey and Pomona in Rockland County. The hills of Harriman Park rise in the distance, and are especially spectacular in the fall.

South Mountain Rd. is an old, windy, bumpy road that takes you under High Tor to Haverstraw on the Hudson. The road starts in a working orchard and passes a vineyard. After you pass a quarry, slow down as you enter a cut in the rock -- the busy intersection of Rt. 9W comes up suddenly, as the view of Haverstraw unfolds.

Next, go through Haverstraw, a quiet old industrial town which provides a change of pace from the fields and woodlands earlier in the ride. The riverfront area of Grassy Point contains a huge factory, but also has several marinas and some interesting small homes and bars right on the river.

Stony Point is a rocky promontory that juts into the Hudson River opposite Verplanck. It is here that General "Mad Anthony" Wayne crept up on the British in 1779 and boosted the Colonial Army's morale with his surprise victory. Today there are fine picnic areas

SADDLE RIVER-STONY POINT
45.9 Miles

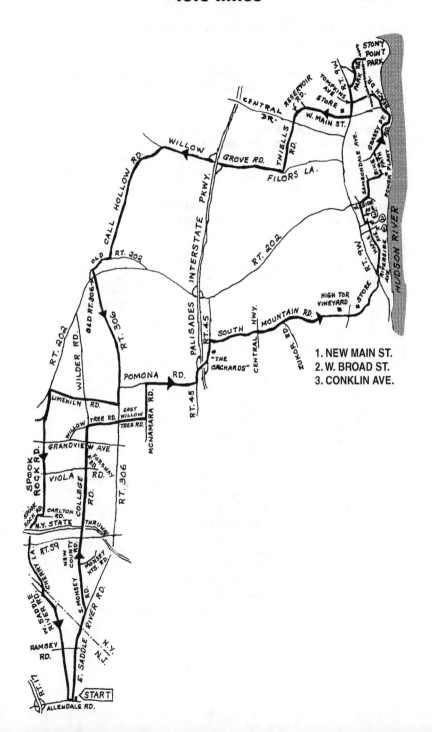

1. NEW MAIN ST.
2. W. BROAD ST.
3. CONKLIN AVE.

overlooking the river, an old lighthouse and lots of wild raspberries to look forward to in July.

The return route takes you through two of the more remote back roads of Rockland (Call Hollow and Spook Rock) before heading back to Saddle River.

Directions to Starting Point: The route starts at the intersection of **Allendale Rd. and E. Saddle River Rd.** in Saddle River. Use the Saddle River/Woodcliff Lake exit off Rt. 17 (about 10.5 miles north of I-80 or 7 miles south of New York Thruway Exit 15). Proceed 3/4 mile toward Saddle River. Parking is available in several shopping centers near the intersection, or on Sundays behind the post office at the intersection.

Pt. to Point	Cume	Turn	Street/Landmark
0.0	0.0		From the intersection of Allendale Rd. and E. Saddle River Rd. (County Rt. 75), proceed north on **E. Saddle River Rd.** (the post office will be on your left)
3.4	3.4		Enter New York State
0.8	4.2	L	**S. Monsey Rd.**
1.2	5.4	S	Name changes to **New County Rd.** (Monsey Heights Rd. goes right)
0.7	6.1	S	Cross Rt. 59. Road changes name to **College Rd.**
1.9	8.0	S	Cross Viola Rd. Road changes name to **Forshay Rd.**
1.3	9.3	R	**Willow Tree Rd.** (street sign is on the left)
0.8	10.1	S	Cross Rt. 306. Road changes name to **E. Willow Tree Rd.**
0.9	11.0	L	**McNamara Rd.** (T)
0.7	11.7	R	**Pomona Rd.** (T)
1.2	12.9	L	**Rt. 45** (T)
0.7	13.6	R	**South Mountain Rd.** (just past "The Orchards" fruit market)
1.7	15.3	S	At blinking light, to continue on **South Mountain Rd.**
0.7	16.0	BL	To continue on **South Mountain Rd.** (Zukor Rd. goes right)
1.6	17.6		**High Tor Vineyards and Winery** on left
0.1	17.7	S	At stop sign (no street sign) to continue on **South Mountain Rd.** Store on left

Pt. to Point	Cume	Turn	Street/Landmark
			after intersection
0.8	18.5	BL	**Rt. 9W**. CAUTION: Slow down as you enter rock cut going downhill: the traffic light at the bottom comes up suddenly!
0.1	18.6	R	At first right, by Tilcon Plant sign, onto **Riverside Ave.** (no street sign)
1.1	19.7	S	Cross New Main St. Road has changed name to **Maple Ave.**
0.1	19.8	L	**W. Broad St.**
0.1	19.9	R	**Conklin Ave.**
0.3	20.2	R	**West Side Ave.** (traffic light)
0.1	20.3	L	**Samsondale Ave.**
0.2	20.5	R	Toward power plant and **W. Haverstraw Recreation Area**
0.1	20.6	BL	Onto **bike route** by power plant
0.3	20.9	S	At end of bike path onto **Beach Rd.** (no sign). Becomes **Grassy Point Rd.** (no signs)
2.0	22.9	R	**Beach Dr.**
0.5	23.4	L	At stop sign under very low railroad underpass onto **Tompkins Ave.** (no sign). Road goes uphill
0.6	24.0	R	**Rts. 9W/202** (T; yield sign). There is a store across the road, to the left
0.3	24.3	R	**Park Rd.**
0.3	24.6	S	Toward **Stony Point Park** (ignore bike route signs, which point left here)
0.4	25.0		Leave bike at bike rack and walk up hill to picnic area and lighthouse. Ride back the way you came after visiting the park
0.4	25.4	S	At yield sign, returning the way you came
0.2	25.6	L	**Rt. 9W** (T)
0.7	26.3	R	**W. Main St.** (traffic light). Store on right after turn
0.8	27.1	BL	**Reservoir Rd.**
0.3	27.4	S	Cross four-lane Central Dr. at stop sign onto **Thiels Rd.**
0.8	28.2	R	**Filors Lane** (T). Road will change name to **Willow Grove Rd.**
1.3	29.5	S	Ride under Palisades Interstate Pkwy.
0.5	30.0	L	**Call Hollow Rd.**
2.9	32.9	R	**Old Rt. 202** (T)

Pt. to Point	Cume	Turn	Street/Landmark
0.3	33.2	L	**Old Rt. 306**
0.1	33.3	S	Cross Rt. 202 at traffic light onto **Rt. 306**
1.5	34.8	R	**Lime Kiln Rd.** (traffic light)
1.3	36.1	SL	**Spook Rock Rd.** (T). CAUTION: Steep hill before this intersection — control speed. Do not turn onto Rt. 202
0.7	36.8	BL	At fork to continue on **Spook Rock Rd.** (Old Rt. 202 goes right)
0.4	37.2	S	Cross Grandview Ave. at stop sign
2.1	39.3	R	At T to continue on **Spook Rock Rd.** (Carlton Rd. goes left)
0.5	39.8	S	Go under N.Y. Thruway
0.2	40.0	S	Cross Rt. 59 at traffic light. Road changes name to **Cherry Lane**
2.0	42.0	L	**W. Saddle River Rd.** (T)
3.8	45.8	L	**E. Allendale Rd.** (traffic light)
0.1	45.9		Intersection of **Allendale Rd. and E. Saddle River Rd**. End of route

RIDES STARTING IN MID-HUDSON VALLEY
(WEST SIDE OF RIVER)

If you rode the Saddle River-Stony Point ride, you looked to the north and saw the start of the magnificent region known as the Hudson Highlands. These storied hills are the feature of three routes in this region, chock full of places to stop, see the sights, take pictures and enjoy the history.

A little to the west lies the fertile farmland of Orange County, which still is ripe for quiet cycling down country lanes where corn and cows are the prominent features. The open farmland of this part of the Mid-Hudson Valley contrasts sharply with the woods and rocky hills of Westchester.

Still further north are two tours centering around the college town of New Paltz in Ulster County, a recreationalists' mecca. ATBers, hikers, rock climbers and cross-country skiers have flocked to the Shawangunk Mountains just west of town for years, and road riders can find fine cycling in the shadow of Smiley Tower, the Mohonk Mountain House lookout tower on top of one of the mountains and visible for miles.

This is a growing part of New York State and is busy with tourists on weekends, but *RIDE GUIDE* shows you the quieter roads and paths to cycle on, while still linking the main attractions of the region.

Two challenging routes start at Bear Mountain Inn — but a good part of the challenge is selecting which of the many points of interest you should spend time at. **Bear Mountain-Harriman** features the hills of Harriman State Park and is particularly beautiful in the fall. A steady climb of over 1,000 feet can be rewarded by a swim in Lake Welsh. Count the lakes on Seven Lakes Drive — the largest, Tiorati, could be in Minnesota with its many islands and channels between them. Another climb up Long Mountain is followed by a 10-mile descent into West Point.

There are so many things to see along **Both Sides of the Hudson** that you could spend three days along the route. Among the highlights are West Point, Storm King Arts Center, New Windsor Cantonment, Washington's Headquarters in Newburgh, Cold

Spring shops, Boscobel restoration and Garrison art galleries. On top of all this are the most breathtaking views of the finest river valley in America -- from the West Point parade grounds, along Old Storm King Highway, on the Newburgh-Beacon Bridge bike path, under Breakneck Ridge, at the Bear Mountain Bridge and countless places in between.

West Point to the Apple Country is a new route for this edition of *RIDE GUIDE Hudson Valley* that takes you north from the military academy along the Old Storm King Highway, then west through Cornwall and to Brotherhood Winery in Washingtonville. From there the route goes around Stewart Airport to head into the apple orchards north of Newburgh. The return route includes an option to cycle over the Newburgh-Beacon Bridge (also the link to the route for train riders from New York) before another breath-taking run under Storm King Mountain. Do this route on a summer Sunday or the Saturday before Labor Day and enjoy the famous outdoor military band concerts at Trophy Point after the ride!

The rolling farm (and becoming suburban) country west and south of Monroe is the destination for **Monroe-Pine Island**. Pine Island is the center of a major onion-producing area, and lovers of this particular vegetable will want to cycle here at harvest time just to inhale the strong aroma. En route, pedal through Sugar Loaf, a working crafts village and Warwick, with its large Main St. homes and small, attractive Pacem in Teris meditation center. On the way back to Monroe, Chester features many antique shops.

Monroe-Montgomery heads north and west to the Wallkill Valley. Among the highlights, besides delightful rural pedaling, are a farm museum, a ski hill with a commanding view, an art gallery with excellent Hudson Valley prints, and a huge photogenic railroad trestle coming out of a mountainside.

New Paltz Figure 8 is for road-riders visiting the capital of cliff-climbing and ATBing. Two loops, which can be combined into one long ride, go through the relatively flat valleys of the Wallkill and Rondout Rivers and Shawangunk Kill for many miles. In between are very quiet, Vermont-like stretches of rural countryside, with the towering Shawangunk Mountains always in view. The Ulster County Fairgrounds are passed; come in August to see a genuine country fair.

For fat-tire riders who can't make it up to New Paltz, **Goose Pond Mountain** is a delightful jaunt near Monroe featuring miles of both single-track and a wide old auto road that pass nothing but abandoned farmfields and ancient glacial forest. This little-known area allows ATBers to get away from it all fast, even though it is right off busy Rt. 17.

Minnewaska State Park is well-known to ATBers from all over the East Coast as *the* place to go. The route presented here, one of many in the park, samples the highlights of carriage path, cliffside views and swimming beach on a remote lake that make this park a fat-tire paradise.

BEAR MOUNTAIN-HARRIMAN - 41.4 MILES

Terrain: This is one of the hilliest rides in the book, yet any cyclists who rides regularly will have no trouble. The hills are long and well-graded, for the most part.

Traffic: Totally dependent on the season and day you ride. Harriman Park roads are quiet most weekdays and non-summer weekends, but can be extremely busy on summer weekends. Off season, Seven Lakes Drive is as empty as a backwoods hiking trail. Long Mountain Pkwy. and Rt. 9W, however, are always busy.

Road Conditions: Excellent. One optional dirt bike path.

Points of Interest: Bear Mountain Park (hiking, zoo and museum); **Lake Welsh** (swimming); **West Point.**

Bear **Mountain** and Harriman State Parks contain 54,000 acres of mountains, woods, lakes and streams. While this area is quite popular on summer weekends, at other times cyclists could easily imagine themselves very deep in the wilderness rather than a short 40 miles from Times Square. Fall is an especially great time for this route because there are so many tree-covered mountains turning colors.

Start at Bear Mountain Inn. Descend to river level, then either climb the shoulder of Dunderberg Mountain with the highway or use the unpaved bike path. The bike path is a better alternative because it provides spectacular views of the marshes near Iona Island.

Turn west at Tompkins Cove, and ride west on Wayne Ave., a pleasant woodsy road named for General "Mad Anthony" Wayne. When you reach Gate Hill Rd., prepare for a long, steady, seemingly endless climb to Lake Welsh (elevation 1,015 feet). A swim feels so good right now!

A wild, fast, curvy roller-coaster downhill takes you to Kanawauke Circle and onto Seven Lakes Drive. The view of Lake Tiorati with its islands is particularly breathtaking. After passing Tiorati Circle, it's a straight, fast, almost four-mile downhill to the big, busy traffic circle where you will begin a three-mile climb up Long Mountain. Busy Rt. 6 has a wide shoulder for this climb.

BEAR MOUNTAIN-HARRIMAN
41.4 Miles

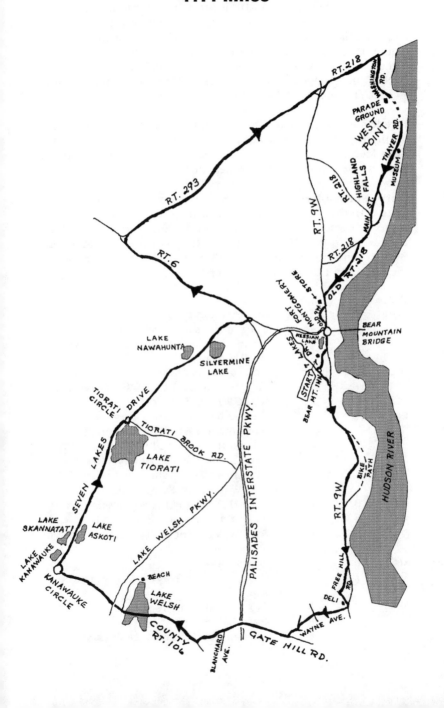

The traffic and climb are worth it because you will then enjoy ten miles of almost continuous downhill or flat terrain into West Point. Traffic is light and there are superb views of undeveloped mountainous land owned by the Military Academy. West Point contains the finest vantage points for river and mountain scenery in the Hudson Valley. Return to Bear Mountain via the homey villages of Highland Falls and Fort Montgomery.

Directions to Starting Point: Bear Mountain Inn is at the northern end of the Palisades Pkwy. and the western end of the Bear Mountain Bridge. Head south on Rt. 9W from the traffic circle where these roads meet. Bear right at the traffic light in 0.4 miles, then turn right into the Inn. There is a parking fee.

Metro-North Directions: (6.3 miles each way from the station). Take a Hudson Line train to Garrison (you may have to change trains at Croton-Harmon). Turn right after detraining, and head up the hill to Rt. 9D. Go south on Rt. 9D to the Bear Mountain Bridge. Cross the bridge, go south on Rt. 9W, then bear right at the traffic light to the Bear Mountain Inn.

Pt. to Point	Cume	Turn	Street/Landmark
0.0	0.0		Start at the south end of the Bear Mountain Inn parking lot. Exit toward **Rt. 9W South**
0.2	0.2	L	Go two-thirds of the way around Bear Mt. Circle toward **Rts. 9W/202 South**
0.7	0.9	BR	**Rts. 9W/202 South** (T)
0.4	1.3		Choose between riding over the mountain on **Rt. 9W** or bearing left to ride on the (unpaved but smooth) old road, labeled as the **Hudson River Greenway Trail**, which will rejoin Rt. 9W at Jones Point in about 2.5 miles
4.8	6.1	R	**Free Hill Rd.** (by Lynch's Restaurant)
0.3	6.4	L	At T and stop sign (no street sign)
0.2	6.6	BR	**Rt. 9W/202 South** (T). Deli on the right at the intersection
0.0	6.6	R	**Wayne Ave.**
0.8	7.4	S	To continue on **Wayne Ave.** (no street sign)
0.6	8.0	R	At stop sign (no street sign)
0.2	8.2	R	**Gate Hill Rd.** (T)
2.9	11.1	BR	No sign (**Harriman State Park** sign on

Pt to Point	Cume	Turn	Street/Landmark
			right shortly after turn). Road becomes **County Rt. 106** at Orange County line
1.9	13.0		Turn right to go to **Lake Welsh beach**
1.7	14.7	SR	At Kanawauke Circle onto **Seven Lakes Drive** toward Lake Tiorati
3.3	18.0		Go halfway around Tiorati Circle to continue on **Seven Lakes Drive**
3.8	21.8		Go seven-eighths the way around traffic circle onto **Rt. 6 West**
3.3	25.1	SR	**Rt. 293**
6.8	31.9	L	**Rt. 218**
0.1	32.0	BL	To continue on **Rt. 218 North**
1.2	33.2	R	Enter **West Point** at Washington Gate. Follow **Washington Rd.** and **Thayer Rd.** past Parade Ground. Where cars are detoured near Catholic Chapel, continue straight by Trophy Point. Walk your bike by barriers near the officers' club and library to continue on **Thayer Rd**.
3.2	36.4		Exit West Point at **Thayer Gate** Go **left** to bypass Highland Falls or **right** to pedal through town
0.7	37.1	S	Both roads meet at fountain. Continue on **Main St. (Rt. 218 South)**
0.7	37.8	BL	Near "Speed Limit 40" sign toward Grace Baptist Church (turn is before Academy Motel) onto **Old Rt. 218**
1.3	39.1	L	**Rt. 9W**
0.8	39.9	BR	**Old Rt. 9W** (traffic light). Store on right after turn
0.5	40.4	BR	**Rt. 9W**
0.5	40.9		Go halfway around circle to continue on **Rt. 9W South**
0.4	41.3	BR	At traffic light
0.1	41.4	R	Into **Bear Mountain Inn** (end of route)

BOTH SIDES OF THE HUDSON - 48.9 MILES

Terrain: Some hills going up and down from the river, but mostly very gentle rollers.

Traffic: Mostly moderate because of the limited number of roads right along the river in this area. Gets a little heavy on Rt. 9D on nice weekends.

Road Conditions: Good, except Rt. 9D in Beacon which is perennially under construction.

Points of Interest: West Point (military museum, parade ground, chapels and views); **Old Storm King Highway** (cliffside road with incredible views); **Museum of the Hudson Highlands; Cornwall-on-Hudson** and **Cornwall; Storm King Arts Center**, a huge modern sculpture garden; **New Windsor Cantonment** (state historic site, a colonial winter camp); **Washington's Headquarters** in Newburgh; riding across the 2-mile **Newburgh-Beacon Bridge; Cold Spring** (shops and riverfront park); **Boscobel Restoration; Garrison** galleries; **Bear Mountain** Bridge, Park and Inn.

The **Hudson Highlands** are as majestic now as when Thomas Cole and other 19th Century artists sat near the river and sketched Storm King, Crow's Nest, Bull Hill and other peaks that rise as much as 1,000 feet from river level. You will catch all the prime vistas as you cycle riverfront roads, one of which is carved into a mountainside.

Thanks to the addition of a bike path on the newer of the Newburgh-Beacon twin spans, it is possible to make a loop trip, enabling you to enjoy different views coming and going. There are so many things to see and do — you could easily spend three days on this route!

Start at Bear Mountain, a park worthy of a day's visit in itself with its inn, zoo, boating lake and miles of fine hiking. Head through West Point. You may wish to divert off the route and visit the chapels and stadium, but the main route (the old auto route, now closed to through car traffic) passes the parade ground and the best view of the river at Trophy Point.

Next cycle the Storm King Highway. This engineering marvel was carved into the side of the mountain in the 1920s using mules and musclepower and reminds many people of Route 1 in California because it curves in and out of valleys high above the water. This road is quite narrow and curvy, so be listening for traffic, which generally is light. Also, if the road is closed due to rockslides, a fairly frequent event in rainy seasons, it should still be available for cycling.

You have the choice of two routes in Cornwall — the main route through town, with its nice homes and shops, or the alternate through the woods, which passes the very interesting Museum of the Hudson Highlands (regional flora and fauna).

Next head to the Storm King Art Center, a major outdoor collection of large-sized modern sculpture with Storm King and Schunemunk mountains as the backdrop. Head into Vails Gate next, where the historic-minded might wish a side trip to a large old house that served as General Knox's headquarters in the Revolutionary War. Two other historical spots in the Newburgh area are passed by the main route: New Windsor Cantonment (the colonial army winter camp in 1782) and Washington's Headquarters.

After cycling through a rejuvenating part of the aged river city, cross the 2-mile bridge to Beacon and drink from a water fountain right on the path. Next, head south on Rt. 9D, climbing toward the base of 1,500-foot Mt. Beacon. A few miles further brings a glorious descent to river level — and awe-inspiring views of Storm King across the way. Tunnel under Breakneck Ridge and head into Cold Spring, a charming village of antique and crafts shop with a classic riverside park, complete with bandstand. Ice cream and other goodies are readily available. Expect large crowds on nice weekends.

A mile south of Cold Spring is Boscobel, a restored mansion with an incredible collection of 18th and 19th Century furniture. The gardens and river view, as well as the house tour, make it worth the admission price.

Finally comes Garrison, a tiny, quaint riverside hamlet with several art galleries and no stores to speak of. This is one town that time truly forgot, although those who saw the movie _Hello Dolly_ might remember the scenery (it was filmed here, even though the story took place in Yonkers).

Historic markers talking about Benedict Arnold's treachery and

BOTH SIDES OF THE HUDSON
48.9 Miles

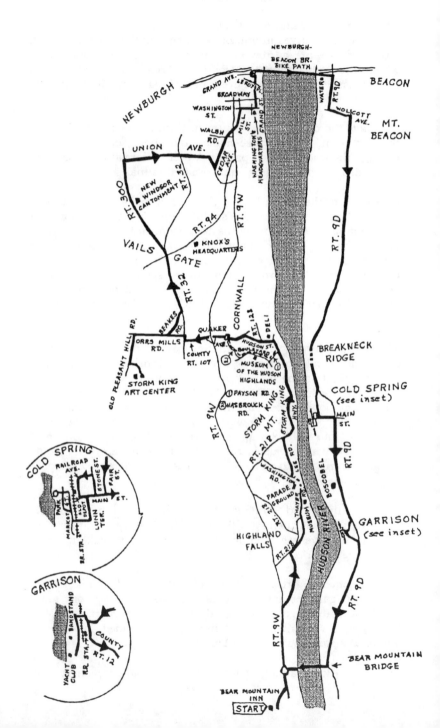

the colonial attempts to chain the Hudson to shut off British ships abound on the final run to the Bear Mountain Bridge.

Directions to Starting Point: Bear Mountain Inn is at the northern end of the Palisades Pkwy. and the western end of the Bear Mountain Bridge. Head south on Rt. 9W from the traffic circle where these roads meet. Bear right at the traffic light in 0.4 miles, then turn right into the Inn. There is a parking fee.

Metro-North Directions: Take a Hudson Line train to Garrison or Cold Spring (you may have to change trains at Croton-Harmon). Join the route at Mile 42.5 or Mile 37.1, respectively.

Pt. to Point	Cume	Turn	Street/Landmark
0.0	0.0	L	Starting in front of the Bear Mountain Inn, exit toward **Rt. 9W North**
0.1	0.1	BL	At traffic light onto **Rt. 9W North**
0.4	0.5		At traffic circle, go halfway around to continue on **Rt. 9W North** toward West Point
1.8	2.3	BR	Toward Grace Baptist Church on **Old Rt. 218**
1.3	3.6	S	At yield sign onto **Main St. (Rt. 218)**
0.8	4.4	BR	At fork toward West Point. Rt. 218 goes left
0.6	5.0	S	Enter Thayer Gate of West Point. You are on **Thayer Rd.**
0.3	5.3	S	Continue straight on **Thayer Rd.** to follow old auto route through West Point (closed to through auto traffic). Turn **left** if you wish to visit stadium and chapels (expect significant climbing!). When you reach barriers near library and officer's club, walk your bike around them and head toward parade ground
1.4	6.7	S	**Parade Ground** on left. Trophy Point (view) on right. Road is now called **Washington Rd.**
0.9	7.6	R	**Lee Rd.** toward Lee Gate. Ignore "gate closed" signs -- you will be able to get through with a bike
0.7	8.3	S	Through Lee Gate (walk bike around gate on right if gate is closed. Restrooms in gate building
0.1	8.4	BR	At yield sign onto **Old Storm King**

Pt. to Point	Cume	Turn	Street/Landmark
			Highway (Rt. 218). Be wary of traffic!
3.8	12.2		If you wish to take slightly hillier alternate route through woods, avoiding most of downtown Cornwall and visiting museum, turn **left** at **Payson Rd**. At T, turn **right** onto **Boulevard. Museum of the Hudson Highlands** will be on your left. Keep going in the same direction after visiting museum. **Bear right** at **Hasbrouck Rd.** which will take you to a traffic circle. Rejoin main route at Mile 13.9
			Cyclists wishing to go through Cornwall, continue **straight** at Payson Rd. intersection
0.2	12.4	L	To continue on **Rt. 218**. Deli on right just past turn
0.3	12.7	BL	At blinking light onto **Hudson St**. Rt. 218 goes right
0.6	13.3	BL	At traffic light onto **Main St.** (no sign). Street goes through downtown Cornwall
0.6	13.9	BR	At traffic circle onto **Quaker Ave.** which passes Grand Union supermarket (on your left)
0.4	14.3	S	Go under Rt. 9W.Road becomes **County Rt. 107**
0.5	14.8	R	**Rt. 32** (T)
0.2	15.0	L	After crossing bridge onto **Orrs Mills Rd. (County Rt. 20)**
0.5	15.5	L	**Old Pleasant Hill Rd.** (toward Storm King Art Center)
0.2	15.7	L	Into **Storm King Art Center** (admission is charged)
0.2	15.9		**U-turn** at building and ride back the way you came in
0.2	16.1	R	At end of driveway onto **Old Pleasant Hill Rd.** (no sign)
0.2	16.3	R	**Orrs Mills Rd.** (T; no sign)
0.2	16.5	BL	At fork onto **Beakes Rd.**
0.4	16.9	BL	**Rt. 32** (T)
1.2	18.1	BL	At traffic light in Vails Gate onto **Rt. 300 North.**
			If you wish to visit **Knox's**

Pt. to Point	Cume	Turn	Street/Landmark
			Headquarters, turn **right** at this corner onto **Rt. 94**. The building is on the right in 0.8 miles at the corner of Forge Hill Rd.
1.2	19.3		**New Windsor Cantonment** (state historic site) on right
1.0	20.3	SR	**Union Ave.**
1.6	21.9	S	At traffic light. Cross Windsor Highway (Rt. 32)
0.7	22.6	L	**Cedar Ave.**
0.8	23.4	S	At stop sign. Cross Walsh Rd.
0.1	23.5	R	At T
0.0	23.5	BL	Cross Rt. 9W then **bear left** onto **Mill St.** (no sign). Cross old bridge
0.7	24.2	R	**Washington St.**
0.4	24.6	S	At traffic light to cross Liberty St. **Washington's Headquarters** will be on your right
0.1	24.7	L	**Grand St.**
0.1	24.8	S	At traffic light. Cross Broadway
1.0	25.8	BL	**Leroy Pl.** (T)
0.2	26.0	R	At bike route sign onto **Grand Ave.** (no street sign)
0.3	26.3	L	Onto **bike route** crossing Newburgh-Beacon Bridge. Water fountain available on Beacon side of bridge, right on the path
2.0	28.3	R	At end of bike route onto **Rt. 9D South**
1.4	29.7	L	At traffic light to continue on **Rt. 9D South**
1.1	30.8	R	To continue on **Rt. 9D**
3.9	34.7	S	Through tunnel under Breakneck Ridge
1.5	36.2	BR	**Fair St.** (no sign; Rt. 9D goes uphill, and Fair St. follows the river)
0.6	36.8	R	**Main St.**, Cold Spring (T)
0.0	36.8	R	**Stone St.** (first right)
0.1	36.9	L	**Railroad Ave.**
0.0	36.9	L	Curve **left** by the tracks — ice cream available in old depot on the right
0.1	37.0	L	**Main St.**
0.0	37.0	R	**Lunn Terrace** (immediate right)
0.1	37.1	R	After crossing railroad, turn **right** at yield sign onto **Market St.** (no sign)

Pt. to Point	Cume	Turn	Street/Landmark
0.1	37.2	L	**Main St.**
0.1	37.3		Turn around at bandstand and park on river and cycle back over tracks following the route you came over on
0.4	37.7	R	**Main St.** (T)
0.3	38.0	R	**Chestnut St. (Rt. 9D South)** (traffic light)
1.1	39.1		**Boscobel Restoration** on right
2.6	41.7	R	Toward Garrison Art Center. Turn is just past a big stone church (on right)
0.4	42.1	L	Cross railroad
0.0	42.1	L	Onto road that parallels river
0.2	42.3		Turn around at the end of the road, by the Garrison Yacht Club
0.2	42.5	R	Over railroad bridge
0.0	42.5	R	After crossing bridge onto **County Rt. 12**. Do not go up hill the way you came down
0.6	43.1	R	**Rt. 9D** (stop sign)
4.6	47.7	R	Cross **Bear Mountain Bridge**
0.6	48.3		Go three-quarters of the way around the traffic circle onto **Rt. 9W South**
0.5	48.8	BR	At traffic light toward **Bear Mountain Inn**
0.1	48.9	R	Into parking lot at **Bear Mountain Inn**. End of route

WEST POINT TO THE APPLE COUNTRY - 53.0 MILES

Terrain: Gently rolling, for the most part. Somewhat hillier in the apple country.
Traffic: Light to moderate throughout.
Road Conditions: Excellent.
Points of Interest: Pretty villages of **Cornwall-on-Hudson** and **Cornwall; Brotherhood Winery**; cycling through apple orchards; pretty old homes of **Balmville** section near Newburgh; **Newburgh-Beacon Bridge** bike path; **river views** from Cornwall Landing and on Old Storm King Highway; **West Point**.

The **Hudson Valley** has traditionally been an apple-growing region, and this ride takes you to the big orchards north of Newburgh, for mile after mile of pleasant riding.

New York State is also a famous grape-growing state, and the Brotherhood Winery, located 17 miles into the route, bills itself as America's oldest winery. If you are there at the right time, the winery people will invite you to take off your shoes and squeeze some grapes in a barrel!

Head out of West Point along Old Storm King Highway, the tremendous cliffside road carved out of the mountainside. Keep an ear out for traffic, as the cliffs tend to muffle car noises. Zoom down into picturesque Cornwall-on-Hudson and then cycle through neighboring Cornwall, with many pleasant shops.

Next ride through beautiful countryside near the Schunemunk Mountains, just west of Cornwall. The mountains are owned by nearby Storm King Arts Center, and are full of excellent hiking trails. Cycle under a huge railroad trestle that comes right out of the mountain.

Brotherhood Winery is located in the town of Washingtonville. It features tours and food, restrooms and gift shops. Next cycle on roads which make a long, lazy circle around Stewart Airport.

Soon the hills will get noticeably longer and steeper. You have entered apple country. If you are here in May, bring your camera to get a shot of mile after mile of white blossoms.

A delicatessen in Middle Hope is a good place to reprovision before the final ride south along the river. Go through beautiful Balmville, which features large homes and large shade trees, including an enormous one right in the middle of the road. For cyclists with extra energy, a ride across the 2-mile-long Newburgh-Beacon bridge is a way to enjoy cool river breezes and great views of the mountains to the south.

The return to West Point features the Newburgh waterfront and Cornwall Landing, a park with spectacular views right on the river. On the hill up for the landing, look for a spring on the left to fill your water bottles.

Finally, return to West Point on Old Storm King Highway. If you are lucky enough to be here on a summer Sunday or the Saturday before Labor Day, stay for the military band concerts at Trophy Point — they are worth hanging around for, and by arriving early and by bike you will avoid the traffic created when thousands of music lovers converge with their picnic dinners. Concerts begin at 8:00, and the Labor Day Weekend concert features the 1812 Overture, complete with real cannons!

Directions to Starting Point: The route begins at **Eisenhower Hall** on the campus of the U.S. Military Academy at West Point. From the end of the Palisades Pkwy. or Bear Mountain Bridge, take Rt. 9W North to Rt. 218 and follow the signs in Highland Falls to the Thayer Gate of West Point. Follow the auto route past the stadium and chapels, then turn right and left to get to the parking lot for Eisenhower Hall, which is a large modern brick building (the performing arts center) under Trophy Point, over-looking the river.

Metro-North Directions: (about 4 miles from station, each way): Take a Hudson Line train to Beacon (you may have to change trains at Croton-Harmon). Ride up the hill to Rt. 9D, then follow Rt. 9D North about two miles to the Newburgh-Beacon Bridge. Cross the bridge, and pick up the route at Mile 41.4. When you reach West Point, cycle the route from the beginning.

WEST POINT TO THE APPLE COUNTRY
53.0 Miles

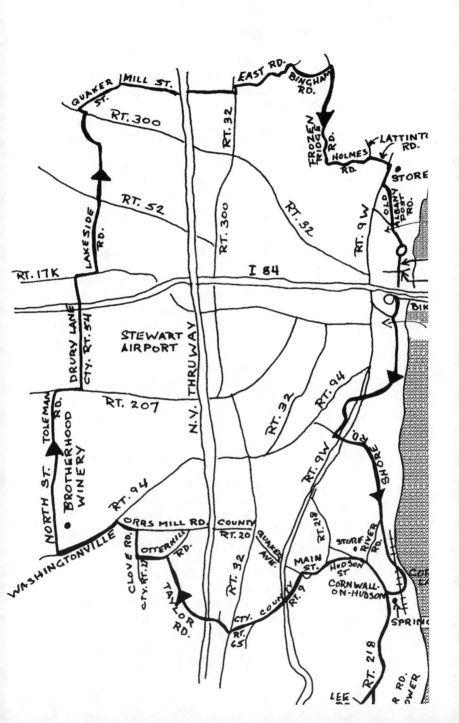

Pt. to Point	Cume	Turn	Street/Landmark
0.0	0.0	R	Exit Eisenhower Hall parking lot toward building with large green awning and turn **right** up the hill on **Ruger Rd.**
0.3	0.3	R	**Washington Rd.** (main road of West Point)
0.4	0.7	R	**Lee Rd.** (toward Lee Gate). Ignore signs saying gate is closed — bikes can get through
0.7	1.4	R	Walk bikes to the right of closed gate and then turn **right** on **Old Storm King Highway (Rt. 218)**
3.8	5.2	L	In center of Cornwall-on-Hudson to continue on **Rt. 218** (deli on right after turn)
0.3	5.5	S	Where Rt. 218 bears right, onto **Hudson St.**
0.5	6.0	L	At traffic light onto **Main St., Cornwall**
0.5	6.5		Go three-quarters of the way around traffic circle and turn onto **Angola Rd. (County Rt. 9)**. Back of shopping center will be on your right. After a short climb you will go over **Rt. 9W**
2.6	9.1	R	**County Rt. 65**
0.9	10.0	S	Use caution approaching busy Rt. 32 (stop sign is at the bottom of a steep hill). Carefully cross Rt. 32 onto **Taylor Rd.** (toward Fish and Game Club)
0.1	10.1	L	To continue on **Taylor Rd.** (cross stream, then go over N.Y. Thruway)
1.7	11.8	L	**Otterkill Rd.** (T). This road will take you under enormous railroad trestle
1.2	13.0	R	**Clove Rd. (County Rt. 27)** (T)
1.0	14.0	L	**Orrs Mills Rd. (County Rt. 20)** (T) (in Salisbury Mills — food available)
0.3	14.3	L	**Rt. 94** (T)
2.3	16.6	R	**North St.** (by Gulf Station in downtown Washingtonville)
0.3	16.9	R	Into **Brotherhood Winery** (not the car entrance, but bikes can get in). After stopping at winery, exit the way you came in and turn **right** onto **North St.**, heading away from Washingtonville.

Pt. to Point	Cume	Turn	Street/Landmark
			Road will change name eventually to **Toleman Rd.**
3.6	20.5	R	**Rt. 207** (T)
0.5	21.0	L	**Drury Lane (County Rt. 54)**
3.5	24.5	R	**Rt. 17K** (T)
1.0	25.5	L	**Lakeside Rd.** (turn is before I-84, by Stewart Airport Diner)
1.6	27.1	S	Cross Old South Plank Rd. (Rt. 52) at stop sign to continue on **Lakeside Rd.**
1.5	28.6	L	At yield sign to continue on **Lakeside Rd.**
0.9	29.5	L	**Rt. 300** (stop sign)
0.1	29.6	R	**Quaker St.**
1.0	30.6	R	**Mill St.** (go under N.Y. Thruway after turn)
1.3	31.9	L	**Rt. 32** (climb)
0.6	32.5	R	**East Rd.**
2.5	35.0	R	**Bingham Rd.** (not far after second "Dawesville" sign)
0.3	35.3	R	**Frozen Ridge Rd.** (climb through apple country)
1.7	37.0	L	**Holmes Rd.** (street sign is hidden — turn is by stone wall and rock before Apple Knolls Estates sign)
1.2	38.2	R	Near bottom of hill, turn **right** onto **Lattintown Rd**. Confusing intersection, in that Lattintown Rd. also goes straight! You will pass a "hill" sign immediately if you've made the correct turn
0.3	38.5	R	**Rt. 9W** (T). CAUTION: Stop sign at bottom of steep curvy hill, go slow! Deli on left shortly after turn
0.9	39.4	L	**Old Albany Post Rd.** (turn is by Balmville Plaza and Honda dealer)
1.0	40.4	L	**Balmville Rd.** (T). CAUTION: Road ends in steep, curvy downhill. Control your speed!
0.2	40.6	S	At intersection with enormous tree in center, onto **Commonwealth Ave.**
0.7	41.3	S	Cross Downing Ave. at stop sign
0.1	41.4		Bike path for Newburgh-Beacon Bridge comes off to the right. It's 2 miles across (and 2 miles back!) for those with

Pt. to Point	Cume	Turn	Street/Landmark
			energy, or for those going to the Beacon train station. If you take the path and are returning to the route, turn **right** at the end of the path to continue
0.3	41.7	L	**Leroy Pl.** (T). Ride along the Newburgh waterfront, going straight at two stop signs
3.6	45.3	L	Onto **Rt. 9W South**. CAUTION — busy road, no shoulder
0.8	46.1	L	After bridge, at blinking light, onto **Shore Rd**. Walk your turn!
0.9	47.0	L	To continue on **Shore Rd**. River Rd. goes right and uphill. You stay flat
0.8	47.8	R	In park by river **(Cornwall Landing)**. Cross railroad tracks and climb woodsy hill. Near the top, look for a spring on the left side of the road, set back in the woods
0.4	48.2	L	**Rt. 218** (T). Note: If you need food, turn **right** and ride 0.4 miles to center of Cornwall-on-Hudson
3.4	51.6	L	At **Lee Gate** (walk bikes around gate) into West Point
0.7	52.3	L	**Washington Rd.** (T)
0.4	52.7	L	**Ruger Rd.**
0.3	53.0		**Eisenhower Hall** parking lot. End of route

MONROE-PINE ISLAND - 46.8 MILES

Terrain: Gently rolling. Some hills, but much easier than, say, northern Westchester or Rockland. Flat as a pancake near Pine Island.
Traffic: Mostly light to nonexistent, except a bit busier into and out of Warwick and Chester.
Road Conditions: Generally excellent. One 0.8-mile flat stretch of dirt road.
Points of Interest: Crafts and arts shops of **Sugar Loaf; Pacem in Teris meditation center** near Warwick (outdoor sculpture garden by quiet stream); **Chester** antique shops.

Open vistas of cows and cornfields, several interesting villages and the East Coast's major onion-producing area are the rewards of this long cycle tour.

The mileage may make this look like an ambitious tour but cyclists of average ability should not have any trouble because the terrain is gentle.

Start outside Monroe at a dirt parking area used by mountain bikers exploring Goose Pond Mt. (see route on page 160). Head through horse farms and creeping suburbanization to Sugar Loaf, a working crafts center that has become a popular weekend tourist spot. The hill giving the village its name, off to the left as you pedal into town, is spectacular to see in the fall.

Warwick has some beautiful large homes on its Main Street. Turning west, pass the quiet and charming Pacem in Teris ("Peace on Earth") meditation center, an outdoor sculpture garden by a stream run by author and philosopher Frederick Franck. Head toward Pine Island on pretty rolling back roads with few cars. The small hamlet of Amity has some interesting old buildings and a photogenic church.

Pine Island has a huge expanse of flat fields with rich, black soil, perfect for growing onions and other veggies. Ride by in late summer at harvest time and the aroma of onions is almost overpowering. The farmer's market has unbelievably low prices on local produce. A large pannier might be advisable to hold your purchases!

MONROE-PINE ISLAND
46.8 Miles

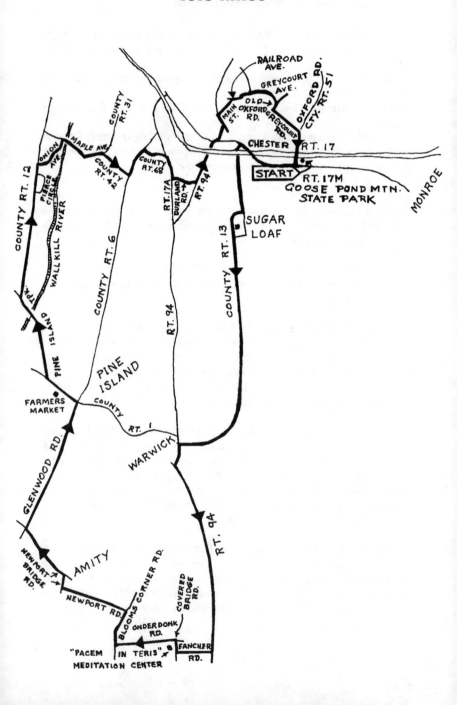

Ride north through more farms (and along Onion Ave., of course). Bypass Florida (Florida, N.Y., that is) and head for Chester. Uptown Chester has some interesting antique shops while historic downtown Chester looks like a Hollywood set - a set of very old storefronts.

Return to Monroe over still more quiet roads paralleling Rt. 17.

Directions to Starting Point: Goose Pond Mt. parking area is located on Rt. 17M. Take Exit 128, Oxford Station Rd., off Rt. 17. Turn right at the end of the ramp and proceed a short distance to the junction of Rt. 17M. Turn left, and the parking lot will be on the left immediately. (No facilities available).

Pt. to Point	Cume	Turn	Street/Landmark
0.0	0.0	R	From Goose Pond Mt. parking area, turn **right** onto **Rt. 17M West**
2.3	2.3	L	**County Rt. 13** toward Sugar Loaf and Warwick (traffic light after going over Rt. 17). After the turn, you will go under Rt. 17
2.5	4.8	R	At sign pointing to **Sugar Loaf**
6.3	11.1	L	**Main St. (Rt. 94)** (T). Cycle through downtown **Warwick**
0.2	11.3	BL	At traffic light to continue on **Rt. 94**
3.2	14.5	R	**Fancher Rd.** (by "Emmerich Greenhouse" sign)
0.4	14.9	R	**Covered Bridge Rd.** (T). **Pacem in Teris** meditation center on left after crossing stream
0.0	14.9	L	**Onderdonk Rd.** (T)
1.7	16.6	R	**Blooms Corners Rd.** (T)
0.9	17.5	L	**Newport Rd.**
1.3	18.8	BR	At yield sign. Road changes name to **Newport Bridge Rd.**
0.1	18.9	L	To continue on **Newport Bridge Rd.** You are in the hamlet of Amity
1.5	20.4	R	At stop sign onto **Glenwood Rd.** (no street sign)
1.9	22.3	L	**Pine Island Turnpike (County Rt. 1)** (toward Westtown)
0.2	22.5		Pine Island Farmers Produce Market on left — check out low prices

Pt. to Point	Cume	Turn	Street/Landmark
0.5	23.0	R	Toward Port Jervis to continue on **Pine Island Turnpike** (store on left after turn)
2.4	25.4	R	Toward Middletown onto **County Rt. 12** (no street sign)
4.7	30.1	R	**Onion Ave.** (next right after Pierce Circle)
0.7	30.8		Road becomes dirt
0.8	31.6		Pavement returns
0.5	32.1	R	**Maple Ave.** (T; no sign)
1.6	33.7	R	**County Rt. 42** (toward Orange Farm)
1.2	34.9	L	**County Rt. 6** (toward Orange Farm and Goshen)
0.7	35.6	R	**County Rt. 68** (toward Orange County Dept. of Social Services)
0.9	36.5	R	**Rt. 17A** (T)
0.6	37.1	L	**Durland Rd.**
0.7	37.8	L	**Rt. 94** (T)
3.3	41.1	R	At T to continue on **Rt. 94 North**
0.2	41.3	L	At traffic light to continue on **Rt. 94 North**
0.2	41.5	L	At T in Chester business district to continue on **Rt. 94 North**
0.3	41.8	R	**Main St.** (sign for historic downtown Chester)
0.3	42.1	BR	**Railroad Ave.**
0.1	42.2	BR	**Greycourt Ave.**
0.8	43.0	R	At intersection just past railroad underpass. Straight ahead is marked as a dead end
0.2	43.2	L	**Old Oxford Rd**. Becomes **Greycourt Rd.**
2.0	45.2	R	At T onto unmarked **Oxford Rd. (County Rt. 51)**
1.6	46.8	L	**Rt. 17M** (T)
0.0	46.8	L	**Goose Pond Mt. parking lot**. End of route

MONROE-MONTGOMERY - 50.2 MILES

Terrain: A few hilly spots, but mostly just rolling.
Traffic: Very light to moderate near Montgomery and Walden and on Rts. 32 and 17K.
Road Conditions: Good throughout. No dirt.
Points of Interest: Orange County **farm and woods** scenery; **Hill-Hold Farmstead Museum**; quiet town of **Montgomery**; large dam at **Walden; Bethlehem Art Gallery** (many interesting Hudson Valley prints); magnificent view of **Schunemunk Mt. railroad trestle; Japanese gardens** at Gasho Steakhouse; **Museum Village**.

If quiet, rural back roads are your fancy, this is an ideal pedal. Head from the growing area of Monroe and Chester toward the still-quiet towns of Montgomery and Walden. In between, enjoy fields, woods, views and serene cycling.

The first point of interest is near Montgomery. Orange County has a huge park here, which includes the Hill-Hold Farmstead Museum and a ski slope. It's worth a side trip to the top of the ski slope for the commanding view of the Wallkill Valley.

Montgomery has some charming small homes on Clinton and Bridge streets. Next head alongside the Wallkill River to Walden, an old industrial town with a large dam visible from the Main Street bridge.

Head south and east adjacent to Stewart Airport. The Bethlehem Art Gallery is worth a stop to see some beautiful prints of the Hudson Valley. They often have a picture of a view you will see a mile up the road — a large railroad trestle coming out of Schunemunk Mountain. Taylor Rd. heads right next to this mountain, a wilderness area owned by Storm King Arts Center and open to hikers.

On the final leg of the trip, you might wish to stop and see the formal Japanese gardens at Gasho Steakhouse (please leave your bikes in the parking lot). Perhaps stop inside and make reservations for a later dinner — the chefs cook it right at your table.

MONROE-MONTGOMERY
50.2 Miles

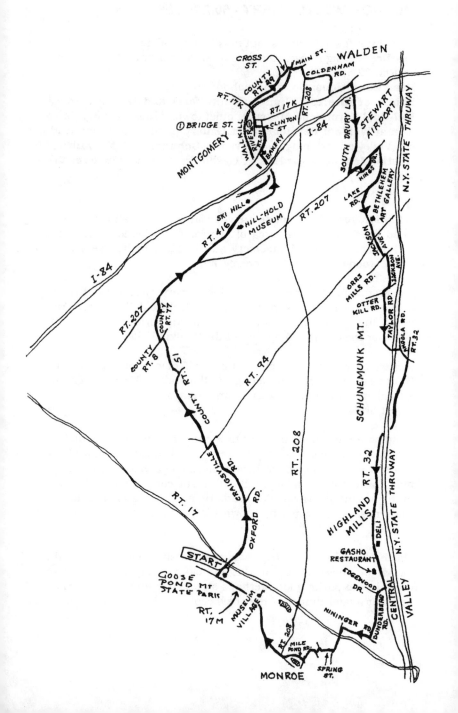

Museum Village, on the final miles of the route from downtown
Monroe to the parking area, is a working restoration of a 19th
Century farm village and worth a look.

Directions to Starting Point: Goose Pond Mt. parking area is
located on Rt. 17M. Take Exit 128, Oxford Station Rd., off Rt. 17.
Turn right at the end of the ramp and proceed a short distance to
the junction of Rt. 17M. Turn left, and the parking lot will be on
the left immediately. (No facilities available).

Pt. to Point	Cume	Turn	Street/Landmark
0.0	0.0	R	From Goose Pond Mt. parking area, turn **right** onto **Rt. 17M West**
0.0	0.0	R	**Oxford Station Rd. (County Rt. 51).** Becomes **Oxford Rd**.
2.1	2.1	S	Road changes name to **Craigsville Rd.** as Oxford Rd. bears right
1.4	3.5	L	**Rt. 94** (T)
0.1	3.6	R	**County Rt. 51**
0.2	3.8	BR	To continue on **County Rt. 51 (Hulsetown Rd.)**
2.1	5.9	L	At curve to continue on **County Rt. 51** (route sign is around the corner)
2.5	8.4	L	At stop sign onto **County Rt. 8**
0.0	8.4	R	Immediate right onto **County Rt. 77**
1.8	10.2	SR	**Rt. 207** (T)
0.4	10.6	L	**Rt. 416**
0.8	11.4		**Hill-Hold Farmstead Museum** on right
0.8	12.2		Turn **left** for county golf course and ski area with beautiful view
2.8	15.0	R	**Rt. 211 East** (T)
1.3	16.3	L	**Clinton St.**
0.1	16.4	R	**Bridge St.** (T)
0.1	16.5	S	At stop sign onto **Rt. 17K**. Cross the bridge over the Wallkill River
0.1	16.6	R	After crossing the bridge onto **County Rt. 29**
3.6	20.2	R	**Cross St.**
0.1	20.3	R	**Main St.** (T)
0.3	20.6	R	At second traffic light in Walden onto **Rt. 208 South**
0.5	21.1	L	**Coldenham Rd./County Rt. 75** (gas station on corner)
2.9	24.0	L	**Rt. 17K** (T)

Pt. to Point	Cume	Turn	Street/Landmark
1.2	25.2	R	South Drury Lane
3.5	28.7	L	**Rt. 207** (T)
0.4	29.1	R	**Station Rd.** and **Church Rd.** (double street sign)
0.0	29.1	L	**Kings Dr.** (T)
0.7	29.8	R	**Rt. 207** (T)
0.4	30.2	R	**Lake Rd.** and **Jackson Ave.** (double street sign)
1.1	31.3	L	**Jackson Ave.**
1.8	33.1		**Bethlehem Art Gallery** on left
0.5	33.6	S	At stop sign. Cross Rt. 94
0.5	34.1	L	**Orrs Mills Rd.**
0.0	34.1	R	Immediate **right** to continue on **Jackson Ave**. Magnificent view of railroad trestle to your right
0.5	34.6	R	**Otter Kill Rd.** (T)
0.1	34.7	L	Quick **left** onto **Taylor Rd.** (T)
1.6	36.3	R	**Angola Rd.** (T; yield sign; no street sign)
0.1	36.4	BR	**Rt. 32 South** (stop sign)
4.9	41.3		Deli on left in Highland Mills
0.8	42.1		**Gasho Restaurant** on right. Beautiful Japanese formal gardens behind restaurant
0.6	42.7	R	At blinking yellow light onto **Dunderberg Rd.**
0.0	42.7	L	To continue on **Dunderberg Rd.** (Edgewood Dr. goes right)
1.3	44.0	R	**Nininger Rd./County Rt. 64** (T)
1.4	45.4	L	At T (no street sign). Cross over Rt. 17
0.6	46.0	BR	At fork onto **Spring St.**
0.7	46.7	L	Toward Business District. Go under railroad underpass
0.1	46.8	R	At T, following signs for Business District
0.3	47.1	R	**Mill Pond Rd.** (traffic light)
0.4	47.5	R	**Rt. 17M West**
1.3	48.8		**Museum Village** on right
1.4	50.2	R	**Goose Pond Mt.** parking area. End of route

NEW PALTZ FIGURE 8 - 28.9, 29.5 OR 58.4 MILES

Terrain: Many long stretches of level river-valley riding, interspersed with rolling hills and one or two good climbs (Cow Hough Road being the biggest).
Traffic: Very light, except moderate on short stretches of state highway and moderate to slightly heavy riding through the village of New Paltz.
Road Conditions: Nicely paved, for the most part (one bumpy stretch near end of second loop, on Old Ford Rd.). ATBers can use the Wallkill Valley Trail, which is a smooth former railroad bed.
Points of Interest: Excellent **views** of the mountains and rivers; **stone houses on Huguenot Street** in New Paltz (one of the oldest streets in the U.S.); interesting towns of **Rosendale** (including mountain caves) and **Gardner** (nice little stores); **Perrine's Covered Bridge** and the **Huterian Bruterhod** at Rifton; **Ulster County Fairgrounds** (fair is at the beginning of August); **Tuthilltown Grist Mill; SUNY** at New Paltz.

This route will give you a well-rounded weekend if you are in New Paltz to hit the ATB trails of Minnewaska State Park. Or it will provide an alternative for your non-off-road-riding companions. Whatever reason you ride it, this course provides fabulous views of the Shawangunk Mountains (without having to climb them!), as well as pedaling alongside or across three area rivers — the Rondout Creek, Wallkill River and Shawangunk Kill. Fat-tire enthusiasts can even go along the Wallkill Valley Trail, formerly a railroad bed, that crosses this route several times.

Two loops are provided, enabling cyclists to bail out in the middle if they so desire. The first loop goes north and east of New Paltz, starting with a tour of Huguenot Street, considered one of the oldest streets in the country and containing many photogenic 18th-century stone homes (tours are given on weekends). The seven miles of Springtown Road are flat and fast, with the 'Gunks always in view to the west. In Rosendale, check out the mountain caves on the left side of Main Street (repositories of corporate records including those of IBM used to be stored in caves similar to these).

NEW PALTZ FIGURE 8
28.9, 29.5 or 58.4 Miles

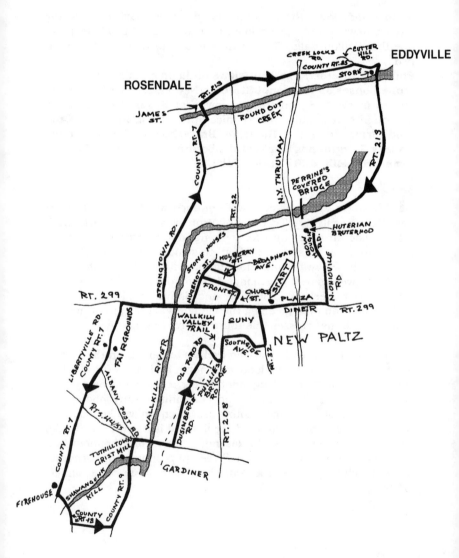

Follow the course of the old Delaware and Hudson Canal along tree-shaded Creek Locks Road. A snack at the deli by the bridge over the Rondout Creek in tiny Eddyville might be welcome. Note the sailboats docked to the left as you cross the bridge — this is the head of navigation on the Rondout, which empties into the Hudson River at Kingston.

Ride alongside a wide lake-like section of the Wallkill River on Route 213 before coming to Perrine's Covered Bridge, very photogenic but not particularly romantic since the New York Thruway hovers overhead. The Huterian Bruterhod across the road is the home of a community of Amish-like people (a bit less wary of outsiders than the Amish) who build beautiful and solid wooden toys, among other things. Return to New Paltz by climbing the hills of Cow Hough Road then zipping through the pretty apple orchards of Ohioville Road.

The second loop goes south and west of New Paltz. It features miles and miles of cornfields and farm country, with the 'Gunks even closer off to the west. Stop at the Ulster County Fair if you're here in early August. Also get off your bike to tour the Tuthilltown Gristmill (open Wed.-Sun.), which has a pretty picnic area by the Shawangunk Kill. Return into town via the campus of the state university, which once hosted a GEAR (Great Eastern Bicycle Rally).

Directions to Starting Point: The **Plaza Diner** in New Paltz is on Rt. 299, New Paltz's Main Street, about 1/2 mile east of N.Y. Thruway Exit 18, on the right hand side.

Loop 1:

Pt. to Point	Cume	Turn	Street/Landmark
0.0	0.0	R	Exit Plaza Diner onto **Rt. 299 (Main St.)** and turn **right**
0.9	0.9	R	**Church St.** (near bottom of hill in center of village, and just before traffic light that is the junction of Rts. 32 and 208)
0.1	1.0	L	**Front St.**
0.1	1.1	S	Cross Rt. 32 at traffic light
0.1	1.2	R	**Huguenot St.** (T) **(stone houses)**
0.2	1.4	R	**Mulberry St.**
0.2	1.6	R	**Rt. 32** (or turn right on Wallkill Valley Trail, before Rt. 32)
0.1	1.7	R	**Broadhead Ave.**

Pt. to Point	Cume	Turn	Street/Landmark
0.1	1.8	L	**Huguenot St.** (T)
0.1	1.9	R	At fork to continue on **Huguenot St.**
0.3	2.2	R	**Rt. 299** (T). Cross bridge
0.2	2.4	R	**Springtown Rd.**
0.4	2.8	BR	At Y fork, to continue on **Springtown Rd. (County Rt. 7)**, toward Rosendale
6.7	9.5		Use caution as you enter double-S curve heading downhill
0.2	9.7	L	**James St.** (T). Cross Rondout Creek
0.1	9.8	R	**Rt. 213** (T)
0.6	10.4	L	**Rt. 32** (T). Food store on left
0.1	10.5	R	Immediate right onto **Creek Locks Rd. (County Rt. 25)**
1.1	11.6		Go under N.Y. Thruway
3.9	15.5	S	At stop sign where Cutter Hill Rd. comes in from left. Road is now called **Canal St.**
0.4	15.9	R	At stop sign, onto **Rt. 213**. Deli and food store at intersection (this is Eddyville). Cross bridge over Rondout Creek. Note sailboats on left that can reach Hudson. Begin climb on Rt. 213
4.1	20.0	R	Curve right to continue on **Rt. 213**
2.3	22.3		**Perrine's Covered Bridge** on right. **U-turn** (do not go under N.Y. Thruway) on **Rt. 213**. Pass entrance to **Huterian Bruterhod** on right
0.6	22.9	R	**Cow Hough Rd**. First right turn. No street sign at Rt. 213 junction, but there is a street sign on the left as you start up the hill
3.6	26.5	S	At stop sign. You are now on **North Ohioville Rd.**
2.1	28.6	S	At stop sign, crossing Old Rt. 299
0.1	28.7	R	At traffic light, onto **Rt. 299 West**
0.8	29.5		**Plaza Diner** on right. End of first loop

Loop 2:

Pt. to Point	Cume	Turn	Street/Landmark
0.0	0.0	R	Exit Plaza Diner onto **Rt. 299 (Main St.)** and turn **right**
1.0	1.0		Cross Wallkill River bridge, exiting New Paltz

Pt. to Point	Cume	Turn	Street/Landmark
1.0	2.0	L	**Libertyville Rd./County Rt. 7**
1.7	3.7		**Ulster County Fairgrounds** (both sides of road)
3.1	6.8	R	At fork, where Albany Post Rd. goes off to the left. Head toward Bruynswick. Still on **County Rt. 7**
1.3	8.1	S	At stop sign, crossing Rts. 44/55
3.7	11.8	L	Onto unmarked **County Rt. 18**, immediately past firehouse (on right)
0.3	12.1		Cross 12-ton bridge
1.0	13.1	L	**Long Lane (County Rt. 18)**
2.2	15.3	L	**County Rt. 9 (Albany Post Rd.)** (T; no street sign)
3.4	18.7	L	Toward **Tuthilltown Grist Mill**
0.1	18.8	L	Toward mill
0.0	18.8		**Mill; U-turn**
0.0	18.8	R	At stop sign
0.1	18.9	L	**Albany Post Rd.** (stop sign)
0.1	19.0	R	**Rts. 44/55 East** (stop sign)
0.5	19.5		Cross bridge over Wallkill River
1.1	20.6	L	**Dusinberre Rd.**, in center of Gardner (where food is available). Or you can turn left on Wallkill Valley Trail and return to New Paltz on it. Take Rt. 299 to the right back to Plaza Diner
1.1	21.7	L	**Phillies Bridge Rd.** (T)
0.1	21.8	R	Immediate right onto **Old Ford Rd.**
0.6	22.4	S	At stop sign, crossing Forest Glen Rd. Road becomes bumpy
1.1	23.5	R	Curve right, to continue on Old Ford Rd.
0.8	24.3		Wallkill Valley Trail crosses. Climb hill
0.2	24.5	L	**Rt. 208** (T; no sign). Down hill, cross river, up hill. Watch for traffic
2.6	27.1	R	**Southside Ave.** (after sign indicating you are entering New Paltz)
0.1	27.2	S	At stop sign. Drive through campus of **SUNY/New Paltz**. Go **straight** at all stop signs
0.6	27.8	L	**Rt. 32** (T; no sign)
0.7	28.5	R	**Rt. 299** (traffic light)
0.4	28.9	L	**Plaza Diner**. End of route

GOOSE POND MOUNTAIN (ATB RIDE) - 8.6 MILES

Terrain: Ranges from rolling to short, steep climbs. Single-track has quite a few short, steep climbs, but the main road is just rolling.

Traffic: This is a quiet off-road area, as yet undiscovered by the ATB mob. You may encounter horses. Dismount your bike and walk past them, as they are easily spooked by pedal-powered machines.

Trail Conditions: The main road, a formerly paved road, retains much pavement or else is slightly eroded. Single-track is in good shape, but muddy in low spots and a bit overgrown as it goes through fields. Watch for logs, rocks and stone walls.

Points of Interest: Gorgeous riding through quiet former farm fields with views of hills and valleys; a stream to have lunch by.

Goose **Pond Mountain** is a state park that rarely appears on tourist brochures about the Hudson Valley because it is considered "undeveloped." This makes it an ideal place to ride your mountain bike, especially if you like miles and miles of quiet trails.

Climb out of the parking area and soon leave the noise of Rt. 17 behind. The terrain is rolling but nothing extraordinary that modern multi-gear ATBs can't handle. The park consists of one main road that goes for 2.7 miles and numerous single-track side trails, all beckoning exploration.

The route given here follows one of those single-tracks across a former farm field, now high grass waving in the breeze (be sure to check your body for deer ticks after your ride, as the grass will tickle your legs). Head toward the Davis Family Cemetery, an old plot being restored by a local Boy Scout troop. The single-track heads down to a swampy area past a beaver pond. Trail conditions at research time were too muddy to continue past the swamp, but if you happen to ride here during a dry time you might find interesting trail beyond where a turnaround is indicated.

The single-track winds its way up and down small forested hills. One can easily imagine how the glaciers from the last ice age shaped the land of this park, with gouged valleys and treed hilltops. Eventually you return to the main road.

GOOSE POND MOUNTAIN (ATB RIDE)
8.6 Miles

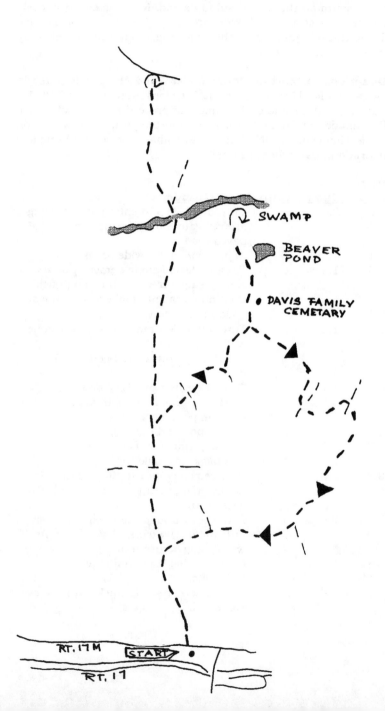

Cycle south on the main road to its end. Near the end is a lovely fast-moving stream to take a break by. If you are not a brave single-tracker, just riding the road is a lovely way to get away from civilization and cars.

Directions to Starting Point: Goose Pond Mt. parking area is located on Rt. 17M. Take Exit 128, Oxford Station Rd., off Rt. 17. Turn right at the end of the ramp and proceed a short distance to the junction of Rt. 17M. Turn left, and the parking lot will be on the left immediately. (No facilities available — be sure to bring lots of drinking water for your ride!).

Pt. to Point	Cume	Turn	Street/Landmark
0.0	0.0	S	Cross Rt. 17M and enter park by going around gate. Go up steep, formerly paved road
1.1	1.1	S	At junction of two wide paths
0.3	1.4	R	Toward Davis Family Cemetery onto skinny single-track path through field. Continue straight at all trail crossings
0.1	1.5	S	Follow red arrow
0.1	1.6	L	Turn left, follow red arrow. Cross stone wall
0.1	1.7	BL	Follow red arrows. Trail gets a little wider
0.0	1.7		**Davis Family Cemetery** on right. Continue straight on path after exploring cemetery
0.1	1.8		Beaver pond on right
0.2	2.0		Swamp; trail often flooded. **U-turn** and ride back up single track
0.3	2.3		Pass cemetery on left. Stay straight (do not go off on path you came in on). Path goes down hill
0.3	2.6		Path goes through evergreen forest on little hilltop. Watch for logs and stone walls going across trail
0.1	2.7		Cross flooded spot. You may have to walk bike
0.2	2.9	S	Cross another single-track path. Go over stone wall.

Pt. to Point	Cume	Turn	Street/Landmark
0.2	3.1	S	Cross slightly wider path. Path then snakes through forested hilltop
0.7	3.8	S	Where wider trail comes in from left
0.1	3.9	L	Into woods at fork. Trail going right goes steeply up hill next to field
0.1	4.0	S	Where several skinny trails go off to the right
0.1	4.1	R	At main trail (T)
0.4	4.5	S	At junction of two wide paths
0.8	5.3		Cross over beautiful stream. Good spot to take a break
0.1	5.4	L	At fork, following slightly wider path
0.5	5.9		**U-turn** at end of road and return the way you came, all the way on the main road
2.7	8.6		Use caution on downhill near end of road. Cross Rt. 17M into parking lot. End of route

MINNEWASKA STATE PARK (ATB RIDE) - 12.3 MILES

Terrain: Moderately hilly. Steady uphill climb to Castle Point, then down, down, down to Lake Awosting.   Return from Lake Awosting is almost entirely downhill.
Traffic: All off-road, but lots of hikers so be careful.
Trail Conditions: Excellent. Some erosion, but mostly very smooth considering the exposure along the cliffs to wind and rain.
Points of Interest: Phenomenal **views** — bring your camera! Incredible **rock formations** such as Castle Point. **Lakes Minnewaska** and **Awosting**, with swimming beaches.

Minnewaska **may have** been a word in the Shawangunk Indian language. But to mountain bikers, Minnewaska means Mecca. Few places on the East Coast can rival this state park's collection of carriage trails, with awe-inspiring views around every corner. Cliffs overlook the Hudson Valley to the east and the big Catskill mountains to the west. Two sparkling-clean lakes — Minnewaska and Awosting — are circled by the paths.   In between are hemlock forests, waterfalls, wild blueberries and lots of rock cliffs.

It's worth the trip to New Paltz, also an outdoor Mecca for rock-climbers, hikers and lovers of the rambling old Swiss-chalet style Mohonk Mountain House, to experience riding at Minnewaska.   This state park used to be the grounds of a hotel rivaling Mohonk, but a fire destroyed the hostelry some decades ago.   The state saved the grounds from development, and although they banned swimming at a famous old skinny-dipping spot under the beautiful Awosting Falls near the park entrance, they are doing a great job maintaining the carriage trails so even novice ATB riders should have no trouble.

Bring your swimsuit — both lakes have beaches with lifeguards. Lake Awosting must be one of the few ride-on beaches, with flat rock slate instead of sand (and that rock extends right into the water, so you can ride right into the lake if you so desire). Be sure to bring lots of drinking water, as there is absolutely no source of drinking water in the park at all.

MINNEWASKA STATE PARK (ATB RIDE)
12.3 Miles

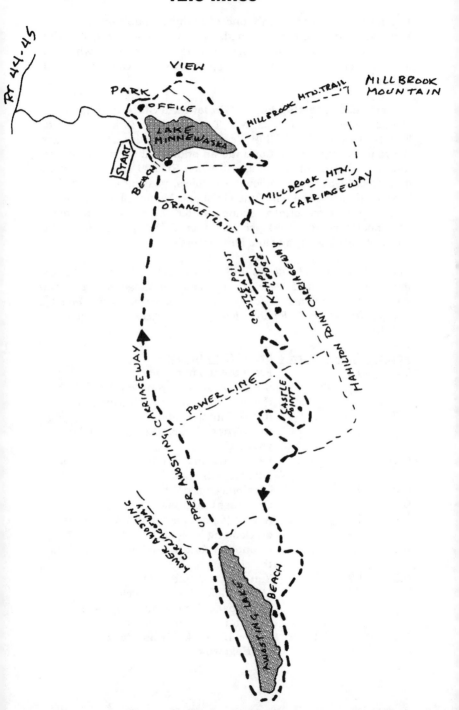

The route described is only one of many available in the park. There are two other carriage roads linking Lake Minnewaska with Lake Awosting, as well as numerous side roads, some of which go miles to achieve yet another tremendous view. Get a map and explore!

Directions to Starting Point: Minnewaska State Park is about 10 miles west of New Paltz, N.Y. Take the New York Thruway to Exit 18, turn left on Rt. 299 West after paying the toll and follow the road through town. Continue an additional six miles up into the Shawangunk Mountains, and when Rt. 299 ends, turn right onto Rts. 44-55 West. Follow for 4 miles, passing en route "The Trapps" (famous rock-climbing cliffs) and Mohonk Preserve (great hiking and cross-country skiing). Enter the park at the main entrance (parking fee $4 per car), then drive up, up, up to the topmost parking lot, by Lake Minnewaska.

Note: Numerous bike shops and other locations in New Paltz rent mountain bikes, and there are a number of motels and bed and breakfasts in the area so you can make a weekend of it. See page 155 for the New Paltz Figure 8 loop for more cycling in the area.

Pt. to Point	Cume	Turn	Street/Landmark
0.0	0.0		From the top of the parking area, with the picnic area on your left, head down the path toward Lake Minnewaska
0.0	0.0	L	At the T intersection, turn left, following the **orange blazes**, keeping the lake on your right
0.1	0.1	R	Past restrooms and diving area, keeping lake on your right
0.2	0.3		Park office on right
0.2	0.5		Go under underpass
0.2	0.7	L	At fork (do not take path toward gazebo overlooking lake)
0.1	0.8	L	At another fork. Enjoy nice view toward the east
0.3	1.1		You're at the bottom of Lake Minnewaska. Prepare to climb switchback. Do not turn onto Millbrook Mountain Trail (a hiking path)
0.2	1.3	L	Yellow-blazed **Millbrook Mountain Carriageway**

Pt. to Point	Cume	Turn	Street/Landmark
0.3	1.6	BR	At fork onto **Hamilton Point Carriageway**, also blazed in yellow (go left for 2.1-mile excursion — each way — to Millbrook Mountain)
0.0	1.6	BR	After slightly eroded downhill, toward **Castle Point Trail** (not toward Echo Rock). Climb
0.1	1.7	L	At T onto blue-blazed **Castle Point Trail**. Continuous gradual climb begins
0.4	2.1		**Kempton Ledge** (view) on left
0.8	2.9		S-curve, climb hill, nice views to left
0.2	3.1		Go under power line
0.8	3.9		Path comes out into open-face cliff. Phenomenal views to left. Watch out for crevice!
0.6	4.5		Emerge at **Castle Point**. See Lake Awosting below and the Catskills off to the West. Downhill ahead!
0.7	5.2	R	At T where Hamilton Point Carriageway comes off to the left. Beware of erosion and "speckled shade" making for some poor visibility as trail continues to descend
0.6	5.8	L	At T, toward Awosting Beach
0.2	6.0		Where trail goes sharp left, go off to the right to see the great view of Lake Awosting. Then return to the trail
0.5	6.5		**Awosting Lake Beach**. After swim, continue straight to circumnavigate lake. Trail is a bit rocky on the far side of the lake
2.3	8.8	R	At fork at end of lake trail. Do not go left onto black-blazed Lower Awosting Carriageway (even though sign says toward parking lot and Rt. 44-55). Cross dam
0.2	9.0	L	Onto green-blazed **Upper Awosting Carriageway**
1.2	10.2		Go under power line
1.4	11.6	S	At junction of orange trail. Continue on **green trail**
0.6	12.2	L	At back end of Lake Minnewaska, by beach (straight ahead of you) and

Pt. to Point	Cume	Turn	Street/Landmark
			restrooms (on right), onto **orange trail.** Keep lake on right
0.1	12.3	L	Toward picnic area and parking lot
0.0	12.3		**Parking area**. End of route